SON
15b —

Are you curious?

'In this powerful and exciting book, Evette Cordy shares the lessons she's learned over a lifetime of helping others to unlock their innate creativity. Combining breakthrough insights, impactful stories and usable tools, Evette masterfully explains how innovation is a learnable process that begins when a life is lived with curiosity.

Applying curiosity in our everyday lives allows us to discover and understand problems more thoroughly. As the first crucial step in the creative problem solving process, problem finding opens the door to innovative and imaginative new solutions.

Readers will find helpful tools for building curiosity skills and living a curious life. This book is definitely not a skim read; you won't be able to put it down after your first peek.'

Dr. Min Basadur - Founder Basadur Applied Creativity, Author of *Power of Innovation, Design-Centred Entrepreneurship* & *Flight to Creativity*

'In this book, athlete, author, and creativity consultant, Evette Cordy, has given us a practical set of exercises comprising a "total body workout" of our curiosity muscles. Cordy quotes Shunryu Suzuki, which sets the tone for a business book that is very Zen.

Cordy's writing is minimalist, well-edited, elegant and spare. She gives us these gifts, modestly and without fluff. She offers something valuable – cultivating these six curiosity mindsets will undoubtedly lead to more innovation and impact in our professional and personal lives.'

Cate Harding - Customer Experience Guru

'Curiosity is, and always will be, a core leadership competency. For those looking to design success into their teams and culture, this book is a great growth hack. A no-nonsense guide to leveraging intellectual curiosity as your secret weapon.'

Campbell Holt - Chief Customer Officer, Mercer Pacific

'As a friend and mentor, I've known for years that Evette has a lot to give. In this book, "Cords" is in fine form. She is magnetic, adventurous, bold and thoroughly disinterested in mediocrity! This book is for use in the home, office, boardroom, or anywhere you please. If you see yourself as a remarkable contributor then apply what you learn.'

Cathy Freeman - Olympic & World 400m Champion, Founder of Cathy Freeman Foundation

'The world is divided into two types of people: those that know it all, and those that are still learning. If, like me, you fall into the second category, then curiosity is the behaviour that you need to adopt to start bridging that gap. This book will start you on the journey of better understanding this critical concept and how to apply it in your business.'

Daryl Bussell - CEO, Luv-A-Duck

'The comedian John Cleese is fond of saying that creativity is a mood. It's not a talent or special skill and it's not related to IQ. It's a practice that takes time and space – "an oasis of quiet for your mind" – where you can explore and play.

In many ways being curious and creative means rediscovering the state of being that comes so naturally to children. "What if we ...", "Imagine that ...", "Let's pretend ..." are phrases that come so easily when we're young, but so much harder when we're grown up.

Cultivating Curiosity is a great resource to help us nurture curiosity in ourselves and in our workplaces. I challenge you to read it, and then be a rebel, a sleuth, or a play-maker. Not only will you make an impact in your business, you might just have some fun along the way.'

Kylie Bishop - Group Executive People & Culture, Medibank Private Health Insurance

Copyright 2018 © by Evette Cordy

First published in 2018 by Agents of Spring, Studio 5,
Level 3, 517 Flinders Lane, Melbourne 3000

The rights of Evette Cordy to be identified as the Author of this Work has been asserted by her in accordance with the *Copyright, Designs and Patents Act 1988*.

All rights reserved. No part of this publication may be reproduced, stored in a retrieval system, or transmitted, in any form or by any means without the prior written permission of the publisher, nor be otherwise circulated in any form of binding or cover other than that in which it is published and without a similar condition being imposed on the subsequent purchaser.

ISBN: 978-0-9953777-6-9

Editing by Kelly Irving
Design by Peter Trigar
Illustrations by Bianca Loiacono

Typeset in Champion and Whitney
Printed in Melbourne, Australia by Whirlwind Print

AGENTS
OF SPRING

agentsofspring.com

A catalogue record for this book is available from the National Library of Australia

CONTENTS

Acknowledgements

The 2016 Fast Company Innovation Conference in New York was the spark that ignited this curious task of writing a book. I have to start by thanking all of the innovative companies, startup founders, CEOs and Angel Investors who attended for setting me on this journey.

More than anything, a big thank you goes out to everyone I have had the privileged opportunity to curiously converse with since this time:

Dr. Min Basadur, Jamie Bunn, P.B., Darryl Bussell, Emily Callaghan, Chris Carroll, Sean Carroll, Kate Cornick, Uday Dandavate, Dave Gray, Cameron Hayes, Barb Hyman, Catriona Larritt, Feyona Lau, Craigie Macfie, Mike McEvoy, Adrian Medhurst, Natalie Mitchell, Catherine Murch (Cathy Freeman), Michelle Parigi, Anne Pengally, Tiz Pittui, Ed Rutherford, Cameron Schwabb, Patrizia Sorgiovanni, Dr. Sivasailam 'Thiagi' Thiagarajan

This book was a personal learning journey for me. Everyone's stories inspired me in so many different ways.

Also, thank you to those who helped me inadvertently, whose ideas and research have informed this book.

Thank you to my amazing editor Kelly Irving, who pushed me to greatness. (Apparently, you need pressure to make diamonds.)

Thank you to designer Peter Trigar and artist Bianca Loiacono (yin and yang), who collaborated to create magic in visualising my ideas.

Thank you to the curious team at Agents of Spring and Agents of Ideas, my current and former clients and colleagues. My involvement with you often involved remarkable learning experiences. Let curiosity always be your guide.

Thank you to my family and friends, who have been incredibly supportive in my notable absence from life outside of work and writing. Hello, I'm back!

Mum and Dad, thank you for nurturing my insatiable sense of curiosity, it has truly been a gift. I grew up thinking that the world of possibilities was only ever limited by my imagination.

Thank you to my amazing husband, father, soul mate, tea maker Troy. You picked up the slack at home and work when things were a little crazy. You allowed me to talk out my thoughts and let me borrow your brain when mine had stopped working.

Finally, thank you to the two most curious little people I have ever known, my precious boys Jasper and Hudson who teach me daily how to cultivate my curiosity as they make sense of the world and test the boundaries of possibility. I love you to the moon and back.

Stay curious.

About the author
Evette Cordy is curious – and she's passionate about making you curious, too.

She is an adventurous problem finder who delivers commercial business growth through breakthrough innovation.

As the chief investigator, lead facilitator and co-founder at Agents of Spring, Evette loves stepping into the shoes of customers to understand the world through their eyes, minds and hearts, and to discover the everyday problems they are facing.

She doesn't stop until she finds the right problem, and then – and only then – does she begin to solve it.

Evette also runs highly interactive and engaging stakeholder and consumer workshops to identify opportunities and facilitate new ways of thinking in organisations and across industries like technology, retail, services, FMCG, property, government, education, and banking and finance.

Evette is not only an innovation expert, but also a registered psychologist with a rich understanding of customer behaviours, motivations and drivers.

She has led innovation projects for the world's leading brands in over 50 countries, a facilitator of LEGO® SERIOUS PLAY® and Creative Problem Solving, and regular leader at the Creative Problem Solving Institute in the USA.

Curious to know more?

agentsofspring.com

Introduction

At a creativity conference I was at a while ago, attendees including me were invited to take part in a team game.

Two teams were assembled and located in separate spaces. Our two teams were handed a ream of paper and given instructions to gain as many points as we could by creating paper planes to hit a target. The target was taped to a garbage can placed roughly five metres away.

There were several rules to the game:

Each plane had to be launched behind a black line taped to the ground.

We had to stand behind the black line when launching the plane.

We had 30 seconds to launch each round of our planes.

No other materials could be used – only the paper.

Every time we hit the target, we would be awarded 10 points. Every time we used a piece of paper, we had to deduct one point. So how might we gain the maximum number of points by hitting the target every time?

We decided we needed our planes to be heavy enough to make the five-metre distance. So we began prototyping, measuring out five metres and creating a mock target.

We quickly discovered we had no control over the direction our planes went. Although they could make the distance, we kept missing the target.

One of our team members suggested scrunching up a piece of paper into a ball, while another suggested adding little wings. We checked with our 'customer' to ensure our prototype would be accepted into the competition, and were given approval (as long as it had wings). We high-fived each other and were pretty chuffed with our innovation, as we believed we had looked at the problem differently and successfully challenged the rules and assumptions.

On our first round, we did okay, scoring 10 points. In round two, we were instructed to create five paper planes. This time we decided to improve our accuracy by scrunching two pieces of paper together. This gave our planes more weight and control.

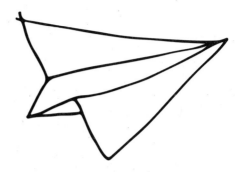

We were excited to see our competitors had not scored across the first two rounds, and we were in the lead. By the end of round two, our accuracy had improved. We scored 40 points. By round three our competitors were still failing to hit the target, and we noticed they were still using the same method from round one (they had made an assumption about what a paper plane must look like), and their traditional paper planes were strewn across the ground. We were well out in front!

But, in the final round, we were asked to construct eight paper planes. We soon discovered that in our excitement, we had used a lot of paper and we only had six sheets left.

We decided to split two sheets of paper in half so we could still construct eight paper planes. We launched our planes but missed the target at least 50% of the time, and we failed to launch all eight planes in 30 seconds.

We had to watch our competitors complete all of their rounds from the sidelines. They were trailing our team by 60 points, but by this time, they had watched what we had done and used that knowledge to improve their planes. Our competitors had a great final round, scoring another 40 points, to only trail us by 20.

After both teams were finished we were asked to hand over the remaining materials we had not used. We had no materials remaining, our competitors counted the sheets of paper left, which came to 14. This gifted them an additional 14 points.

We won – but only by six points.

As we debriefed about the game, the facilitator asked us about the assumptions we had made about the process and our curiosity and creativity around the problem we were trying to solve. Both teams felt they had been very clear on the challenge, which was to maximise the number of points to win.

'Sure,' he said, 'you were very curious about challenging the rules around the paper plane, but you failed to challenge the rules around the launch area. There was nothing to stop you from moving the launch line forward, or the target back.'

Therein, lies the premise of this book.

So often we get intent on solving a problem – sinking all our time, energy, and often money into it – only to discover later on that the answer was much simpler than we thought.

With hindsight, we understood that it didn't require all those resources, meetings or discussions, it just meant looking at a solution that was right in front of our faces.

Take this example of an Australian blue-chip organisation that I was called in to work with.

One of its products had been successful and generated billions of revenue, but over the last two years the product had declined by over 20%. This was a result of increasing competitive pressures as well as new innovative entrants to the market.

The ecosystem surrounding the product was also problematic. The product was difficult to manage through its retail stores and customer service required an overhaul and simplification. The responsible product manager was keen to address the decline by developing a customer-centred solution to better address customer needs and wants. (I'm sure you can relate to this.)

The head of research had made some assumptions about the problem:

1. The product team knew what they were doing.

2. There was nothing new to be found, which was based on experience working on a similar problem.

3. Time was of the essence – the team needed a solution to be in market by next quarter.

4. The involvement of the product team had to be minimised – they were already busy enough.

5. Overseas companies had solved similar problems before, so the team could use a similar approach.

So the organisation went ahead and tested out ideas based on the above assumptions, without spending any exploratory time defining the right problem to solve. Even when I suggested they observe and talk to the employees selling the product on the frontline, they said that wouldn't have much to offer.

I found myself frustrated by this interaction, this lack of curiosity, to dig deeper and truly get to the bottom of the problem. The organisation had a business problem, but what was the customer problem?

Just like my team who became so excited about our scrunched-up prototype that we failed to look at our problem differently, this organisation failed to fully explore the problem they needed to solve.

And this organisation is not alone.

Every organisation is busy, but ask yourself are you busy solving the right problems, the most valuable ones?

There are hundreds, thousands, of companies, of all sizes, all over the world spending millions of dollars implementing new ideas to address the wrong types of problems, just so they can 'get ahead'.

Sure, in today's business world it's important you stand out and stay ahead of your competition, but that is becoming increasingly harder to do. Especially if you're a large organisation that is not as agile as a smaller startup encroaching your space.

You may be investing resources, effort and money coming up with innovative ideas for 'business problems' you don't really have.

The real problem is that you might not be spending enough time understanding what your 'customer problem' is.

You can probably articulate your business problems – falling revenues or portfolio decline – but what are the customer problems you are trying to solve? And how do you find it?

These questions are your key to growth and competitive advantage.

They are the secret to innovation.

The sweet spot lies between a business problem and a customer problem – a solution that you can commercialise, which consumers actually want or need.

The answer is to first problem find, not problem solve.

You've got to flip your thinking and your approach to problems to think and act like your customers. You have to take a walk in their shoes.

You need to learn to be curious about the world and about everyday events in much the same way children are.

This book will show you how.

You'll learn:

How to first become a problem finder, not a problem solver.

Why curiosity is the key to innovation and getting ahead.

What six curiosity mindsets you need in today's business environment.

How to ask WHY about everything – from the way your coffee is served to the types of light fixtures you have in your office.

How to implement lessons from real CEOs, business professionals, experts and even athletes who actively integrate curiosity into their daily lives.

I wrote this book because finding problems is at the heart of who I am and what I do. I believe that problems represent opportunities, and I love the transformative effect of finding problems and reframing them into possibilities.

That is what this book will help you do, too.

It's time to stop solving problems and get curious about finding them instead.

PART 1 – WHY
FIND – DON'T SOLVE

'I'm Winston Wolfe, I solve problems.'

The Wolf, *Pulp Fiction*

In the TV series *Kitchen Nightmares*, famous Scottish chef Gordon Ramsay goes to a restaurant to solve the owner's biggest problems and turn around their failing kitchen.

Ramsay begins each episode meeting the owner and touring the restaurant to understand what is going on, but most importantly, he spends time observing the restaurant in action.

In his observations, Ramsay identifies all kind of problems. The list is usually exhaustive and long, and can range from too many items on the menu to rotting food in the fridge.

In one of my favourite episodes, Ramsay heads to Scottsdale Arizona, USA, to Amy's Baking Company, run by husband and wife team Sammy and Amy.

On the surface, the kitchen looks good. The cakes on display are beautifully presented and Ramsay is greeted by friendly restaurateurs. Upon inspecting the spotless kitchen (which is very unusual for the show) Ramsay declares it as 'clean as a doctor's surgery'. Ramsay tastes the dessert and comments, 'If all your food is as good as your dessert, there is something not quite right here.'

When queried about why Amy's Baking Company needs help, Amy tells Ramsay, 'There are lots of online bullies and haters that come here and attack us. We are the only restaurant that stands up to these people, because they say things that aren't true.'

What's the problem?
If you took all of this information so far on face value, you would assume the restaurant had an issue with its customers. The problem you might therefore try to solve is: **How do we transform our customers' opinions of us?**

Yet, Ramsay's delving uncovers something else entirely.

We discover that the only front of house server on staff, Miranda, is not allowed to input orders into the POS device, pour wine or handle money. The only person who can do that is Sammy, and Sammy doesn't do this well. He often forgets to input menu items. Furthermore, Miranda does not receive tips – they all go to Sammy.

Meanwhile in the kitchen, Amy will only cook one ticket at a time. Consequently, customers wait up to an hour and a half for their food to arrive. When a man comes to the counter to complain that he is still waiting, Sammy screams at him and tells him to wait, otherwise pay and 'f*ck off'. (Do you want to eat at this restaurant now?)

Ramsay sits down to eat his meal. The Fig and Prosciutto Pizza arrives first. He is not impressed by the sweetness but is more concerned that the dough is raw. Ramsay asks Sammy to let Amy know he is unhappy. However, Sammy is worried Amy will walk out if she hears the truth, as she doesn't cope well with criticism, so instead tells her everything is okay.

After 75 minutes Ramsay is served the Blue Ribbon Burger, containing everything but the kitchen sink (mushrooms, blue cheese, marinated, garlic aioli, white truffle oil, crispy bacon bits, and a soggy bun full of grease). The meat is not cooked medium-rare as requested and Ramsay describes it as, 'just a mess, over-complicated, so unnecessary, a disaster, really disappointing'. He goes on to label his next dish as tasting like 'dry cat food'.

It turns out that Amy's Bakery Company has 65 items on the menu to choose from (65!). The dishes are designed to offer everyone something they will like. So as a result of not thinking about whether they could even cook the recipe well or not, the restaurant failed to please anybody at all.

As Ramsay observes an evening service, he watches countless meals being returned and thrown in the bin uneaten. Yet no one giving Amy this feedback. There is constant yelling of profanities at staff, which results in one team member getting fired for simply asking a question.

So what was the real problem?

There were multiple problems that emerged: the culture, customer service, food quality, food service design and timely delivery of dishes. These problems had nothing to do with customer behaviour – in fact, you really couldn't blame them for their bad reviews given none of their needs were being met.

This is a classic example of how in business we launch into solving problem X, without first slowing down to explore if the problem is really Y.

In a 2017 *Harvard Business Review* article 'Are You Solving The Right Problems?' a survey of 106 C-suite executives across 17 countries, uncovered that 85% strongly agreed or agreed that their organisations were bad at problem diagnosis. Plus 87% strongly agreed or agreed that this flaw carried significant costs.

Fewer than one in ten executives believed they were unaffected by the issue. Author Thomas Wedell-Wedellsborg remarked, 'The pattern is clear: spurred by a penchant for action, managers tend to switch quickly into solution mode without checking whether they really understand the problem.'

We launch straight into solution finding without spending the effort to figure out what the real problem is. We jump ahead and try to solve what might not be a problem in the first place. When things aren't going well in our business, our instinct is to 'fix' whatever we perceive to be the problem, as quickly as possible.

If we don't take the time, like Ramsay, to dig deep, to observe and figure out what is really going on, then we throw time, money and resources into something that will fail to have any impact on our business at all – except wasted time, money and resources.

How can you solve a problem, or expect things to change or grow in your business, if you don't know what the real problem is?

The problem with problems

The word 'problem' is seen as a negative, something to be avoided, often even feared.

That's why we try to solve problems too quickly or, worse yet, avoid problems entirely instead of seeking them out. Just like Sammy and Amy did.

Amy was confident in the quality of her dishes, yet she had never left the kitchen to observe her customers eating her food or to speak to them about what they really thought of it.

Rather than telling Amy the customers didn't like the food she was serving, Sammy threw uneaten plates of food into the bin to preserve harmony.

Amy was afraid of failure, so she refused to take accountability for customer feedback. She instead blamed reviewers and bloggers; 'They made up lies to say our food was disgusting'.

Amy was short-term focused, so she was more worried about getting the next dish out than listening to any feedback that might improve their business.

Sammy and Amy were comfortable with doing things how they always did them. Even if that meant keeping 65 items on their menu and not being able to cook any of them well.

Through poor management and unprofessional communication, Sammy and Amy had turned over more than 100 staff in eighteen months.

Sammy and Amy did not want to listen to any advice Ramsay had for them. In the end they let their egos get in the way of turning around their business. After more than 100 episodes of *Kitchen Nightmares*, this was the first episode in which the restaurateurs failed to take ownership of their problems. They subsequently went out of business.

They were not curious about identifying what problems they needed to solve. They were not curious about the opportunities that would be possible if they were open to change.

Albert Einstein was once asked, 'If you have one hour to save the world, how would you spend that hour?' He replied, 'I would spend 55 minutes defining the problem and then five minutes solving it.'

That's exactly what we must learn to do. We must focus our energy on problem finding and to look at problems differently.

ARE YOU LIVING A KITCHEN NIGHTMARE?

If you want to improve your organisation so you can innovate and grow, then check that these four things are not holding you back:

1. You are so close to your daily business that you can't see your problems, or you may even be so used to the problems you normalise them as everyday occurrences.

---

2. You know there are good problems to find, but you don't want to admit what they are – and sometimes people in your business are scared to tell you.

---

3. You are focused on a problem to solve, but it's the wrong one or an ill-structured, ambiguous or undefined one, and you jump far too quickly to solutions.

---

4. You have good problems to solve, but they are related to your current situation, and you are not looking forward to potential future problems.

What's your golden egg?

We often think of problems as a crisis. In Chinese, the word 'crisis' is represented by two characters that translate into the words 'danger' and 'opportunity' – two very opposite meanings. An interesting way to look at it, don't you think? This shows there are both positive and negative perspectives in any problem.

So rather than regarding problems as burdens to be avoided, we need to learn to value problems – to treat them as 'golden eggs'.

The term 'golden egg' was discovered in Japan by applied creativity researcher Dr. Min Basadur. It describes the right problems to solve. (Because let's face it, we can't solve every single problem we find.)

There are always lots of problems to find and solve within a business, but you need to find and solve the problems that represent the biggest growth drivers – the golden problems.

As part of Basadur's research at Toshiba Corporation he was told:

When we hire new scientists and engineers, we keep them out of R&D for two years. Instead, we place them into the sales department to begin their careers. We want them to learn that their job is to learn the problems of the customer. We want them to know we are not going to hand them problems to solve. We want them to know that innovation begins with finding problems to solve.

Businesses that teach their employees that problems are golden eggs recognise that this is the path to innovation. Problems are the secret to identifying business growth drivers, and opportunities are the solutions.

So if you want to be a disruptive innovator at work, if you really want to grow your business, you first need to be a great problem finder.

FOCUS GROUPS ARE LIKE FIGHT CLUB

Remember Marla Singer (Helen Bonham Carter) from the movie *Fight Club*? She attends support groups on testicular cancer and anything else she can find because they are cheaper than a movie and offer free coffee.

The artificial environment of a focus group attracts all kinds of people – and often the wrong types of customers – for all sorts of wrong reasons. Yet this is an organisation's default approach to finding and solving problems.

I am often approached by organisations that want me to moderate focus groups for them so they can 'observe' their customers behind one-way mirrors, like they are the latest zoo attraction. More often than not, these organisations can't even tell me what the problem is that they are trying to solve.

Using focus groups to observe your customers and decipher their problems will do nothing but create more problems for you down the track.

The fundamental issue with traditional focus groups is that people don't do what they say.

Sometimes people lie because they want to appear socially desirable, acceptable or perhaps they are embarrassed. Or sometimes people have good intentions to do something, but it doesn't translate into behaviour that matches their intention.

Have you ever told someone you are going to drink less alcohol and drink more water for a month, for example? What was the result? How did your actions differ from your intentions?

As human beings, we are often not even conscious of our own behaviour.

Focus groups lack context and rely on self-reported behaviour. But the real issue is that focus groups are an easy option for most organisations. They are comfortable and familiar – most don't realise that there is another, much better, way.

In today's business world, you need to be able to walk in the shoes of your customer. To find clues and collect artefacts that build a whole picture of your customers' experiences. That means sitting with them in their lounge room, shopping where they shop, drinking where they drink or eating where they eat.

You must spend time discovering their hopes, fears and values, and viewing the world through their eyes. Noticing what delights them and observing their irritations, frustrations and pain points.

You need to curiously observe what people say, and what they do, and seek to understand deeply what matters to them.

This is the best starting point to finding the right problems to solve.

The richest insights come from observing and actually talking to people in their natural environment.

The value of finding customer problems

Perhaps you are thinking there are enough problems in your business. Why would I want to find more?

Figure 1.1 shows that when you value problem finding in your organisation, your ability to identify growth opportunities increases and so does the value of your business.

Problem finding is a skill. The better you get at this skill, the further you move from being closed to curious. Identifying the right problems will unlock the future growth drivers of your business – and that's what you want, right?

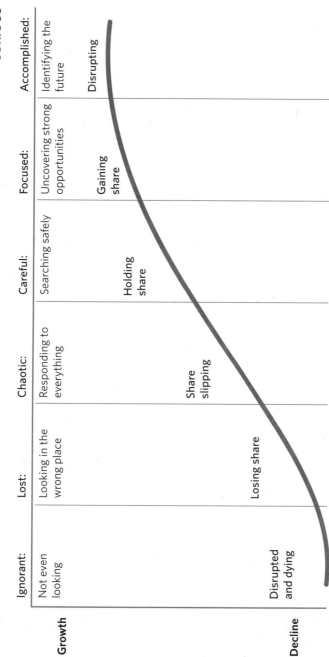

Figure 1.1: The value of problem finding

As you read through each stage, think about where you are at now and where you want to be.

1. IGNORANT: not looking

Are you even looking for problems in your business? Or have you closed your mind and just buried your head in the sand like Kodak did when they ignored digital technology.

If you're at this stage, then it's likely you consider problems as a negative – you don't see them as an opportunity. You go about your daily business as you always have done and believe what you are doing is sufficient. You only respond to a problem when it throws itself at you, which means that you are always fighting fires and never breaking into new ground or territory.

Staying in this situation is madness! How can you ever expect to grow your business if you're not willing to change your behaviour and look for real problems that might help you get ahead? Instead, your business growth is in decline, it's dying – fast.

2. LOST: looking in the wrong place

If you're lost, then you might be making some effort to look for problems, but you are looking in the wrong places.

Your assumptions or anecdotes about customers are likely leading you astray. You have become blinkered in your approach, which means you probably don't know as much as you think you do about your business, customers, operations or competitors.

You're losing market share as you go around and around in circles trying to make what you think might be a breakthrough.

3. CHAOTIC: responding to everything

This is where you only really start looking at or thinking about problems when they hit. By then, it's already too late. Competitors like Amazon are coming into your market, whether you are prepared for it or not.

You are not concerned about trying to find problems to solve, you feel like you have too many to solve already. You are so busy reactively responding to problems that you don't feel you have time to go looking for more.

Your market share is slipping. You are drowning in all of these problems to solve and finding it hard to retain your market position.

4. CAREFUL: searching safely

Here you are looking proactively for problems, but you have only been looking carefully within the context of your current offerings and existing customers. For example, you are trying to modify an existing product or service, when in fact, customers' needs require a completely new solution.

You carefully explore the current issues, challenges and problems you are facing, and your customers' major complaints or difficulties, but you're not looking beyond what you know.

You are holding market share but this is not going to help the future growth of your business.

5. FOCUSED: uncovering strong opportunities

Problem finding is embedded in the culture of your business. You have a deep understanding of your current and potential customer problems. You are looking outside your current industry for broader problems to solve.

You are looking for problems in the context of potential offerings and markets. You are focused on problem finding in the right areas, where you dedicate energy to this practice and appreciate the importance of it.

Your disciplined practice of problem finding is helping you to identify strong opportunities and you are gaining market share.

6. ACCOMPLISHED: identifying the future

This is the Holy Grail. You are looking for problems with lead users and customers of tomorrow. You have a good understanding of the problems today and in the future. You are always on the lookout for the problems that will emerge in five or ten years' time – not just today.

You are looking at how customer needs will change over the coming few years. You see how all of the current disruptions will feed into one another. You are thinking about the biggest problems or pressures that you are likely to face over the next few years.

The future is happening for you in slow motion and you are one of the major disrupters in your market.

An invitation for new thinking

So now you know why you need to see problems as opportunities, and what value there is for your business when you do. Great! Now how do you set yourself up to become an accomplished problem finder. One who can find problems now and in the future and can identify growth drivers that will disrupt your competitors and market?

It starts with three words: **How might we...?**

The words you use to define a problem influence your ability to solve it.

As a simple example, read aloud the following two sentences:

The bill is confusing.

How might we help customers understand our bills?

Each of these acknowledge the same problem – a confusing bill. However, the first sentence is a statement of fact, a fixed reality or even a complaint. Whereas, the second sentence is a question that invites solutions.

Using 'How might we ...?' enables us to reframe our problems into a question, an invitation to seek out the solution.

Remember Dr. Min Basadur who helped us to see problems as golden eggs? In the early 1970s, Basadur was working as a company-wide creative problem solving consultant at Procter & Gamble in the USA, when he got a call from a team in product development.

'We need some help', Basadur remembers the team leader telling him.

For six months, the team had been struggling to come up with a product that could beat Irish Spring, a new and popular green-and-white striped soap bar from Colgate, that had a TV ad showing a man in a meadow, showering with the soap and feeling totally refreshed.

Irish Spring was revolutionary – within a year of its launch it became a billion-dollar business. So as Colgate's market share rocketed, Procter & Gamble knew it was only a matter of time before its market share declined.

The Procter & Gamble product development team had

already tried six times to come up with a soap bar, in all different shades of green, none of which beat Irish Spring in a blind test of consumers. The company had a rule that they wouldn't launch a product unless it could beat a competitor or incumbent in a blind test.

The team was losing confidence, so Basadur organised a full-day, problem finding session. He started with the problem the team had been working on for six months, which was to create a better green-striped soap bar.

Then Basadur asked another question: 'Why might we want to make a better green-striped bar?'

The team's answer was that they'd lost market share.

'Why else might we want to create a better green-striped bar?' Basadur continued. He encouraged his colleagues to think from a consumer's perspective.

One team member volunteered, 'We'd like to make people feel more refreshed.'

'That was the aha moment – we had redefined the problem. That was the secret to the process,' explains Basadur. This led the team to define their problem as: 'How might we make a more refreshing soap bar?'

The team settled on this problem statement and that afternoon generated several hundred possible ideas to the question. Out of the session came the solution to create a bar that reminded people of the beach or the sea coast.

Procter & Gamble launched its soap bar called Coast, which featured swirly blue stripes, after it beat Irish Spring in the blind test.

It only took the team a day to have a creative breakthrough, thanks largely to Basadur and his use of three words: **How might we ...?**

You can still find both Coast and Irish Spring in the market today — along with many similar products from competitors.

The question starter 'How might we ...?' has since spread to some of the most successful companies in business today including Facebook, Google and Ideo.

The Procter & Gamble product development team had originally wasted six months in their innovation efforts. They tried to define the problem too narrowly, jumping too quickly to solutions because they were fixated on green stripes. Now I'm sure you can relate to something like that in your own organisation, right?

HOW MIGHT WE ... ?

So how might we apply this line of questioning and reframing in your own industry or organisation?

Let's look at some problems in the taxi industry, as an example:

Taxis often smell or are unclean.

You never know how long a taxi will take to show up.

We waste time paying with cash or credit card at the end of a ride.

Well, let's face it, finding problems with the taxi industry isn't hard (that's why Uber has been a huge customer success). So if you are a competitor in this space, you might ask:

How might we provide customers with a cleaner, fresher (non-smelly) ride?

How might we inform customers on how long they have to wait for their ride?

How might we make ride payments faster?

Now think about your own organisation or industry.

1. What do you and the people within your organisation already know about a problem or challenge you have?

2. What are 10 different ways you can rewrite this problem using the question 'How might we ... ?' to look at it from different angles?

3. Which one is your most valuable problem?

4. How might you approach your problem differently?

Reframe what you see

A car is travelling on a deserted country road and blows a tyre. The occupants of the car go to the boot and discover there is no jack. They have no mobile reception and even if they did, they are so far out of town they wouldn't get access to roadside service.

They define their problem as, 'Where can I get a jack?' They look about, see some empty barns, but no one is there. They recall that several kilometres back they had passed a service station. They decide to walk to the service station to get a jack.

While they are gone, a car coming the opposite direction also blows a tyre. The occupants of this car go to their boot and also discover there is no jack.

They define their problem as, 'How can we raise the car?' They look around and see, adjacent to the road, a barn with a pulley for lifting bales of hay to the loft. They move the car to the barn, raise it on the pulley, change the tyre and drive off.

This example from psychologist Jacob Getzels shows how the way we frame problems can make them more or less difficult. That is, we can increase our ability to solve problems by reframing what the problem actually is.

Problems do not always present themselves in a way that is clear or when there is an obvious solution. As educational pioneer John Dewey believed: 'A problem well-defined is half solved.'

So look at your problem from as many different angles as possible. To help you do that now, ask yourself the following questions about your business or your customers:

What are our customers' major complaints or difficulties?

What issues, challenges or problems are we facing?

What customer needs will change over the next few years?

What will be our biggest problems over the next few years?

What new pressures might we face in the future?

What problems are experienced by customers and/or other organisations in adjacent/analogous industries?

Your answers to these questions will give you insights into other ways of looking at what you think your problem is. Just try it and see.

A curious problem

How have the world's greatest inventors such as Albert Einstein, Thomas Edison, Marie Curie, the Wright brothers and Steve Jobs had such a big influence on our lives? What is it they have that we don't?

These inventors had an insatiable desire and inquisitiveness of the mind to want to know more, to explore beyond the obvious, and to explore the boundaries of possibility. Quite simply, they were curious.

Todd Kashdan, clinical psychologist and author of the book *Curious*, describes curiosity as the function that urges us to explore, discover and grow. My own definition of curiosity is: **The drive to unearth insights.**

CURIOSITY IS THE TOOL WE USE TO FIND PROBLEMS.

It is only by finding the right problems – not the ones you think you have, or the ones told to you by your customers – that you start to grow, push new boundaries and innovate.

As psychologist Abraham Maslow once said, 'In any given moment we have two options: to step forward into growth or to step back into safety.'

Which one would you rather do?

RECOGNISE
– NOT REWARD

'I think, at a child's birth, if a mother could ask a fairy godmother to endow it with the most useful gift, that gift should be curiosity.'

Eleanor Roosevelt

Which animal has a fingerprint that is indistinguishable from a human fingerprint? (CLUE: it's not a monkey ...)

Don't Google the answer just yet. Let's first assume you don't know the animal, but you are somewhat curious about it.

What is going on in your mind as you think about what it might be? Are you recalling places or parts of the world you have travelled to? Are you thinking about interesting animals you've seen, touched or experienced before?

Now, how does it feel to be curious about the answer to this question? How does it feel while you're searching for what it might be? Does it bug you that you don't know the answer? Is it a bit like an itch that you want to scratch? Or do you feel excited? Is it fun figuring out what the answer might be?

This is what it is like to be curious.

This question shows you how your curiosity is sparked. It's likely you now feel energised to go out and seek more information about the question posed (so go on, Google it – I know you want to).

Curiosity is at its peak when we don't have any information and we want to fill that hunger with knowledge.

Scratch your itch

Curiosity is like the compelling urge to scratch an itch. It makes us want to seek out more information – it makes us want to find problems.

Behavioural economist George Loewenstein developed the Information Gap Theory of curiosity in the 1990s. He believes curiosity is a critical motive that influences behaviour and that arises when we feel a gap exists 'between what we know and what we want to know'.

You are more likely to seek out information if you are curious about something because that's how you 'scratch your itch'.

In a neuroscience study by Loewenstein, participants were asked to:

1. Read a quiz question.

2. Rate how curious they were to know the answer.

3. Rate how confident they were that they knew the answer.

4. Provide an answer.

During the tasks, participants' brains were scanned using functional magnetic resonance imaging (fMRI). The results reinforced Loewenstein's Information Gap Theory, showing that curiosity increases to a point as knowledge increases and then drops off. The effect of perceived knowledge looks like Figure 2.1.

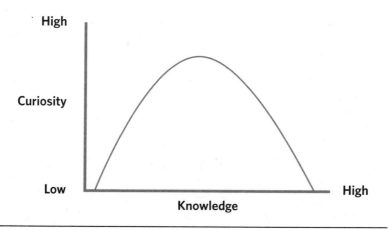

Figure 2.1: Curiosity versus knowledge

This means you can stimulate curiosity by creating a gap between what you know (or think you know) and what you want to know. Just like you saw in the last chapter, sometimes you might not think you have a knowledge gap until you are shown a different way of looking at a problem.

You need to search for problems in different places or outside of your current offerings. Are you curious about what the world will look like in five, ten or 15 years' time? What problems might your customers be facing then?

In order to identify the most valuable problems and future growth drivers of your business, you must first stimulate your curiosity to become a good problem finder.

How might you spark curiosity in your business by creating a knowledge gap?

Curiosity is the fuel for inquiry, learning and discovery – that's why it's critical for organisational growth and innovation.

SNICKERS REALLY SATISFIES

Daryl was once a shift manager for the global family-owned confectionary company Mars at its Australian factory in Ballarat, Victoria. This factory is where household chocolate favourites like Snickers®, M&M'S®, Mars®, Maltesers®, Pods®, Bounty® and Milky Way® are manufactured. The 35-billion-dollar company is owned by John Mars and his siblings, who inherited the business from their father.

Every year, John Mars would travel to Australia to visit the local operations and meet with his associates. On one such tour, John identified an issue in the factory and challenged the team to find out what it was within 24 hours. He offered a $5 reward if the issue could be found.

Daryl was always up for a challenge so happily accepted. He described the whirlwind 24 hours following, 'We went around the factory and must have changed 20 things, found 20 different small issues.'

The next day when John came into the factory, Daryl and his team shared their discoveries and the results from their problem finding exercise and were rewarded with a $5 note. This got framed and put on the wall; however, everyone (including Daryl) remained in the dark as to what the original problem was that John had found.

'We suspect we may not have found the exact issue,' says Daryl. 'He was just challenging us to be better.'

What John Mars did that day was show his employees that they always need to be on the hunt for problems to solve. He opened their minds and eyes to look at their familiar work environment in new ways.

When was the last time you did something like that for your employees? Do you encourage your team to open their eyes and minds in the familiarity of your everyday workplace?

If not, it's time you do.

A curious mind

Curiosity is a state where you anticipate an intrinsic cognitive reward. When we are curious, our brain lights up. We feel good! Curiosity stimulates the pleasure and reward system of the brain.

Cognitive neuroscientist Dr. Matthias Gruber and his colleagues conducted an experiment in 2014 to better understand the effect curiosity has on the brain. Participants were asked to rate how curious they were to learn the answer to a series of trivia questions. Their brains were scanned while they were exposed to the questions and waited 14 seconds for the answer.

The experiment revealed that the more curious a person is to see the answer to a question, the more their brain activity lights up the parts of the brain that regulate pleasure and reward - that is, the dopamine circuit or the wanting system.

Interestingly, this circuit in the brain also lights up when we get extrinsic rewards such as money or treats. Think about a kid in a candy store or anticipating your annual bonus payment.

And yet, we are not rewarded for being curious at work.

If you were given one hour to solve a problem, how much of that hour would you spend on problem finding versus problem solving?

(My guess is that it wouldn't be 55 minutes like Einstein was said to spend.)

Future-focus your outlook

The challenge of every organisation is the incredible pressure placed on short-term results, the intense task-focus of hitting monthly, quarterly, and yearly numbers of revenue and profit targets. Even when a business is delivering year-on-year, double-digit revenue growth, it's expected that you do everything to sustain that performance.

In a short-term environment, there is always a deadline looming. Organisations are always chasing results, which creates a culture of 'doing'. So, when a business problem arises it is common for organisations to run with that problem, and quickly jump to solution finding and implementation.

This results in fast, cheap solutions that do not last long and do not have much impact for your customers.

Being motivated to find and solve your customers' biggest problems (the ones they often don't even realise they have) is the heart of innovation, and it takes longer than you currently think.

Being innovative involves doing something new or different that creates value for your customers and clients. Creating value means helping customers get from where they are today to where they want to be tomorrow.

It's a future skill you have to harness within your organisation to ensure that you keep up with this demand. And curiosity is the key to that skill.

Before innovation comes problem finding, and before problem finding comes curiosity. You need to learn to cultivate curiosity within your organisation if you want to encourage better problem finding. You need to do the heavy lifting.

You need to get smart about the problems you give time, resources and money to.

That means creating the space for curiosity to thrive within your business now as well as in the future.

The benefits to business are big – when you nurture curiosity in your team, you find problems, solve problems and identify breakthrough innovation in your organisation.

Cultivating curiosity is a no-brainer

In a 2017 *New York Times* article, LinkedIn identified curiosity as the second most sought-after soft-skill behind communication, and ahead of adaptability, teamwork and empathy.

Remember, science also proves that it feels good to be curious. We are intrinsically motivated to seek out information and are physiologically rewarded when we stimulate our curiosity. So cultivating curiosity in our organisations really is a no-brainer.

Traditionally, there was a view that leaders should have all the answers for everything, the solutions for every problem an organisation would encounter. That's why they are at the top, leading the organisation. But the reality is that they often don't (they are human, after all).

If leaders create an environment of curiosity they will inspire their employees to ask questions, to learn, and to seek problems and solutions for themselves. When we are curious we are open to discovering new things and this leads to better insights and platforms for problem finding.

As Daryl Bussell, CEO and leader of the successful Australian agribusiness Luv-a-Duck demonstrates:

I always encourage my team that if you're going to work an eight-hour day, try and get your job done in seven hours and 30 minutes. Use 30 minutes a day to go and network, talk to people and other team members, to find out about them, what their pressure points are, ask a couple of clarifying questions that you haven't been able to ask otherwise. Create some time in your day for curiosity.

Most of us won't do that. We feel like if we're not actually 'doing' the tasks allocated to our job, then it means we're slacking off or we'll be seen as being lazy.

But the people that I think are the most successful are the ones who create those windows of opportunity to build a few more connections and to have curiosity about other people's jobs in the business.

EMBRACING CURIOSITY IS A NO-BRAINER

– it makes people feel good and leads to growth and innovation.

AN INSIGHT INTO YOUR CUSTOMERS

Customer insight provides a deeper context to your customers, behaviours, motivations and their problems to be solved.

I believe a good customer insight inspires solution finding and combines:

1. Fact – An observation of how people behave or what they do.

2. Need – An understanding of what sits behind an observation (these could be functional, social or emotional needs).

3. Problem – An issue, frustration or challenge which causes a friction or tension in someone's life.

The bigger the point of pain in a customer's life, the greater the opportunity to create value and an ultimate solution to meet this unmet need.

Let's revisit the taxi industry to put this into context:

1. Fact – I take a taxi to get to my destination.

2. Need – I need to get there fast.

3. Problem – Taxis are smelly, I never know if they are going to show up in time, and I waste time at the end of a trip paying and waiting for a receipt.

Insight statement

'I take a taxi to my destination because I need to get there fast, but taxis are smelly, I never know if they are going to show up in time, and I waste time at the end of a trip paying and waiting for a receipt.'

When you read this insight statement, you can see the friction and it compels you to want to come up with ideas and solutions to solve this person's problem. When you read a good insight, you want to respond with 'Yes that's true. I recognise this'. Good insights inspire people to take action about the problem to solve (like Uber have done for the above).

Only curiosity can lead us to the discovery of insight.

AN INSIGHT
=
FACT
+
NEED
+
PROBLEM

Are you open to it?

So the question really is, how do you learn to cultivate curiosity in yourself and in your organisation?

First, you must be willing to step into the unknown. After all, if you believe you know it all, you won't learn anything new. As American musician Frank Zappa once put it, 'A mind is like a parachute. It does not work if it is not open.'

We are all born with some degree of curiosity, but we also have the ability to foster our curiosity when we are open and committed to seeking out new knowledge, as Figure 2.2 shows.

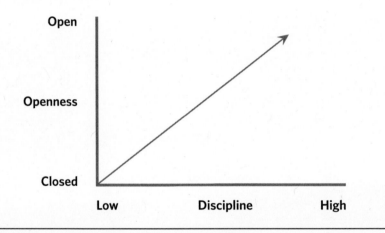

Figure 2.2: Cultivating curiosity

If you are closed to new knowledge you may pre-judge a problem because you think you already have the answers or have seen it all before. Perhaps you believe you should already know what you need to know. You might be fearful of heading into unfamiliar territories, and therefore unwilling to ask 'silly' questions. Or, you might be so busy doing your day job you don't feel you have the time or energy to be open to exploring anything else outside your current scope of work.

In contrast, if you are open to new knowledge, you will see relevance in everything. You will be genuinely open to experiencing curious moments. To learning, enquiring and discovering new knowledge within your business, the way it works, the people, and most importantly understanding your customers' needs and their problems.

If you make little or no effort to be curious, being open will only get you part of the way. It's like beginning a fitness program, it might feel strange and hard work at first, but by dedicating regular practice you can improve and cultivate your curiosity.

If you are disciplined, you make an effort to learn, inquire or discover something new, and you work hard at it. Curiosity takes commitment, effort and persistence. You exercise curiosity more consciously in your daily experiences, making time for curious moments. By doing so, you transform routine tasks, reviving them with new energy and opportunities for discovery.

Sparks of inspiration come from the most unexpected people or places, so practise keeping your mind open.

Openness to experience is often referenced in psychology literature as one of the Big Five personality traits of human beings. Historically, it was believed that personality was a stable characteristic that did not change over our lifetime. However, in the last decade a number of scientific teams have shown through longitudinal research that our personalities – including how curious we are – can change over time.

I first took a Big Five personality questionnaire almost 20 years ago, while I was studying my Masters in Organisational Psychology. Recently I took this questionnaire again, which revealed my openness to experience had increased markedly over that significant period of time.

There is scientific evidence that repeated experiences can change our brains – this is often referred to as 'neural plasticity' – and what this means is our personalities are malleable. We can become more or less open if we choose to. As you go about your everyday life, you have an opportunity to be open to new knowledge and experiences, and the more you practise this then the more open you become.

As American jurist Oliver Wendell Holmes once said, 'A mind stretched by a new idea never shrinks back to its original proportions.'

Practise the practice

Once upon a time I was a professional 400m hurdler. To become an athlete, I knew I needed discipline. This meant prioritising my training and competition ahead of other things that could occupy my time and energy. Running and training had to occupy a place in my everyday schedule. I worked with one of Australia's best track and field coaches, who had coached several Olympic medal athletes. I wanted to give myself the best chance I had to win.

My training was precise. Each week I completed three weights sessions, four track sessions, one hurdle technique session and three core body strength sessions. I followed a concept called periodisation, which relates to program design and requires a level of consistency in your training program. The goal with periodisation is to maximise your gains, while also reducing your risk of injury and the staleness of the practice over the long term by varying the session intensity and frequency.

What this meant was although I consistently used the same building blocks (i.e. track sessions, weights, circuits, hurdle technique), no training session was ever the same. I constantly looked for ways to get the edge to improve my performance and achieve my next personal best. If I had just followed exactly the same program every year, I would never have improved.

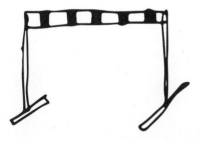

This is the mindset and approach you must have to improve your curiosity and be able to find your most valuable problems to solve.

Not everyone is destined to be an Olympic medallist (I certainly wasn't). However, just like an athlete you can become more curious through disciplined effort. You first need to prioritise the time and energy for curiosity and be disciplined in your approach and mindset.

You can cultivate curiosity by working hard and training your brain, just like we do with exercise, by adopting a curiosity mindset and making curiosity a focus in your business.

As Uday Dandavate, CEO and Founder of global design research firm SonicRim teaches his employees:

Every client project is an opportunity to go meet a bunch of people and get to know their life, which is not like your life. While answering your clients' questions, also learn something for yourself. When you have a genuine personal curiosity for understanding someone else's life, your body language, your aura, everything changes, and the way they respond to you also changes. So that's the core capacity to enjoy your work, and at the same time also benefit from it personally.

So above all else, remember curiosity is all about having a learning experience!

This is exactly what you're going to learn how to do in Part 2 when we look at the six mindsets you need to cultivate curiosity and identify growth drivers in your business.

AN EPIPHANY

Curiosity nurtures life, just as –

The winds nurture life by blowing from high to low pressure areas

The rivers nurture life by flowing from the mountains to the plains

The birds, bees and animals nurture life by migrating from the terrains of low resources to high from cold climates to the warm

Curiosity nurtures life by drawing the mind

>   *from ignorance to knowledge*

>   *from apathy to empathy*

>   *from lethargy to energy*

>   *from status quo to change*

>   *from scepticism to optimism*

>   *from despair to hope*

>   *from dogmatism to openness*

>   *from stagnation to growth*

>   *from a mundane state to the creative*

Curiosity helps builds capacity to thrive amidst ambiguity, complexity, unpredictability and unfamiliarity.

Uday Dandavate, CEO and Founder of global design research agency SonicRim.

CURIOSITY CHECKPOINT

So just how curious are you now? This self-assessment will help you to identify what kind of mindset(s) you have right now and which one(s) you might need to nurture.

There are six mindsets and six corresponding questions to answer to determine how you currently rate in each mindset.

Instructions
First, rate yourself on the following questions using a scale of 0 to 10, where 0 is not at all and 10 is extremely.

1. REBEL
How prepared are you to go out on a limb to seek a better way of doing things? 8

2. ZEN-MASTER
How often are you fully present? 7

3. NOVICE
How comfortable are you when you don't have all the answers? 3

4. SLEUTH
How likely are you to notice things beyond the obvious? 7

5. INTERROGATOR
How likely are you to ask questions that have never been asked before? 7

6. PLAY-MAKER
How open are you to experiencing new things and learning through play? 8

Now mark your responses for each question on the hexagon below. The centre of the hexagon represents 0 and the outside point of the hexagon represents a 10.

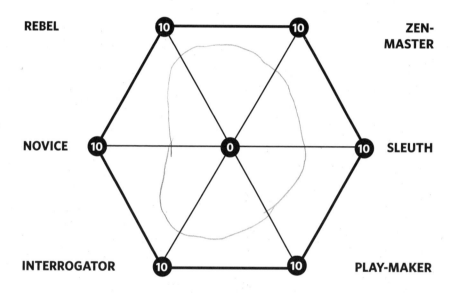

Draw a line between each of your marks and shade the inside area. This is your unique curiosity footprint.

Use your unique curiosity footprint to guide you into Part 2. You could read each of the six chapters in order, or you may choose to start with the mindsets that you feel you are strong on, or those you have identified you need to work on.

AS YOU READ, REMEMBER, YOU CAN USE THESE MINDSETS IN TWO WAYS: to guide and cultivate your own curiosity, and to guide and cultivate the curiosity of others within your organisation.

PART 2
MINDSET 1
REBEL

'If you feel safe you are not doing the right thing.

You need to step out into the water and when your feet are just past not being about to touch the ground, that is where magic happens.'

David Bowie

Let's imagine you are one of seven participants in the Line Experiment study that was first demonstrated by psychologist Solomon Asch.

You are shown several cards and on each card there will be several lines, like those shown in Figure 3.1. Your task is to look at the line on the left and determine which of the three lines on the right is equal to it in length. Sounds simple, right?

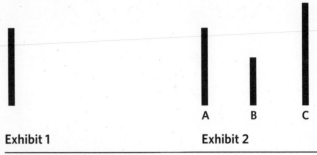

A   B   C

Exhibit 1   Exhibit 2

Figure 3.1: Line Experiment

You are seated sixth in the study, where all but one participant will have to call out their answer before you.

The study begins. Everyone agrees that line A is the same length as the reference line on the left. You think this task is too easy!

The study continues until something unexpected happens. The first participant appears to call out the wrong answer. You start to question whether there is something wrong with their vision. But then everyone else before you clearly fails to call out the correct answer too. What is happening?

Now it's your turn. You are sure that everyone has called out the wrong answer, but it's odd that they all agree on the same one. What do you say?

Chances are you will conform and call out the incorrect answer, just to agree with everyone else.

Results of this original Line Experiment study found that 76% of participants conformed at least once to the wrong majority answer. The other participants in the study were instructed to call out the wrong answer on purpose to see what would happen.

In a 2013 follow-up fMRI study, the participants caved in to peer pressure 41% of the time. These results support the hypothesis that brain regions classically associated with perception can be altered by social influences.

Someone else's view or opinion

CAN ACTUALLY AFFECT WHAT YOU SAY OR DO, OR HOW YOU PERCEIVE THE WORLD.

Imagine how often this happens within your organisation? Have you ever found yourself in a meeting with a strong view on the topic of conversation, completely disagreeing with what is said, yet you sit there and nod your head in agreement? Or perhaps you have been in a conversation where an alternative view to yours has been expressed and you find yourself changing your view?

Most of the time, we don't decide to agree with the other person because our perception has been changed. We go along with it because we don't want to stand out. We fear failure, being wrong, looking silly or getting embarrassed. We fear we might lose our job or miss out on our next promotion.

But at what cost does this come to our curiosity and our ability to find our most valuable problems?

Do you play it safe?

Charles Darwin agonised for two decades (and in fact suffered from debilitating anxiety) over his beliefs on the theory of natural selection. He was unsure how this would be received and what effect this would have on his reputation.

It wasn't until competitor Alfred Russell Wallace, a respected fellow scientist, laid out a similar argument for evolution that Darwin chose to publish his theory. Darwin was incredibly curious, but it took him two decades to be brave enough to share his findings with the world. In today's business environment, curiosity is a competitive advantage. But you can't wait around for your competitors to figure it out before you.

Most of us spend 99% of our time at work playing it safe, following the rules, processes and protocols. This structure and order in an organisation is there for good reason. Any deviation from the norm is usually seen as negative, risky, or as dangerous to the integrity of the organisation. We are scared of standing out or going it alone.

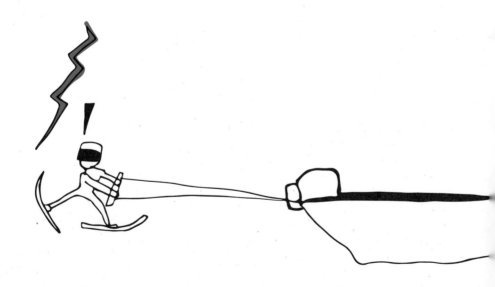

You don't find problems worthy of solving

by playing it safe or following the rule book.

To nurture curiosity, you need to be brave and embrace fear. You must step into the unknown, out of your comfort zone. Fear is what builds boundaries. Curiosity breaks them. This is the very foundation you need to identify the future growth drivers of your business.

Emily Callaghan, Design Officer at 3M, says:

If we want to be catalysts or innovators, if we want to help influence others, then we have to be willing to lead change and challenge the structure of the paradigms. That takes courage. In this space of innovation, of creative problem solving, I really believe it is up to every individual that's in on the team to really own what it means to take this forward. To not just be a participant, but to be an enthusiast.

Humans love comfort. Research tells us that under pressure we prefer familiar options. For example, if you are running late for a meeting and you know that the normal route you take is going to be congested, you are still more likely to take that route because it is what you always do.

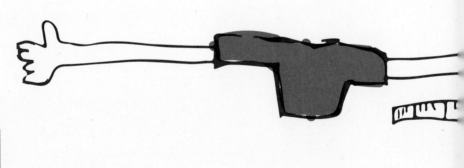

If you always do what you always do, you will always get what you always get.

You will only ever unlock problems worthy of solving if you stretch yourself beyond your comfort zone, if you rebel. It is in this 'stretch zone' where the magic happens and opportunities arise.

As Chris Carroll, CEO, Australia and Southeast Asia, at Widex, puts it:

Leaders and boards of big Australian corporates generally don't have this mentality because they're often lawyers, accountants and black-and-white people who are there to manage risk – which is okay, as long as it's not at the expense of innovation.

Curiosity is grey, a whole load of grey. A lot of people don't like grey. It's uncomfortable, because it's not a number. Or it's not a clause in a contract.

Remove these things, and a lot of us feel very nervous. At C-Suite level there's a lot of personal brand, pride and credibility that we know can be undone very quickly. So we keep away from unsafe territories. But that's when curiosity gets stifled.

You have to place some bets – you just have to.

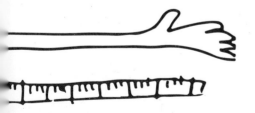

BOLD IS BETTER

In the retail branch network of the National Australia Bank there has always been a focus on selling to customers. Branch staff incentives were tied to sales metrics.

Head of NAB's Customer Strategy, Ed Rutherford, started to question this approach. He pondered what would happen if all the sales metrics were replaced by a single service metric – Net Promoter Score (NPS), a tool used to gauge the loyalty of an organisation's customer relationships.

When Ed first pitched his idea to the person in charge of the retail network, the response was a resounding no. Given the importance of achieving sales targets, it was deemed too risky.

So Ed remained focused on other projects at hand, but he says, 'There was this kind of compelling itch that I needed to scratch. I was curious.'

Boldly, Ed continued to push his idea. 'I really want to try this,' he explained. 'Let's just do this safe-to-fail kind of experiment. Let's just try it.'

Though Ed wanted it to be bigger and technically measureable, he needed to go from a pilot mentality back to an experimental mentality. He realised it didn't need to be perfect and it didn't need to be scalable, that ultimately his team were there to learn.

The trial ran for six weeks and was tested in one branch. During the trial, another bank publicly committed to removing the regulatory environment and sales-based metrics from their frontline retail staff. So this reinforced the importance of the project they were working on. Suddenly, Ed's idea went from a loosely structured skunkworks project to something a lot more senior people were watching.

The result? The experiment was extended for another six weeks. That particular retail store was one of the top three branches in Australia to grow its NPS. At no point did sales dip. If anything, sales increased ever so slightly while staff engagement rose significantly.

This story shows that adopting a rebel mindset to boldly make space for curiosity enables you to find a better way of doing things.

Challenge the status quo
So how do you adopt a rebel mindset? Start by challenging the status quo.

How often do you ask the question: 'Why is this done this way?'

Many practices within organisations are a result of routine and legacy decisions.

Take Joanna Hoffman, for example. She once attended a lecture at Xerox PARC in California, where she got into 'a heated discussion' with Apple expert Jef Raskin about what computers should look like and how they should improve people's lives. Raskin was so impressed with Hoffman that he asked her to interview for a position at the company.

Hoffman accepted and began the Macintosh project in October 1980. She wrote the first draft of the Macintosh User Interface Guidelines and went on to run the international marketing team that brought the Mac to Europe and Asia. She later followed Steve Jobs to NeXT as one of its original members.

In the book *Steve Jobs* by Walter Isaacson, it is revealed that Hoffman had a reputation at both Apple and NeXT as one of the few people who could successfully engage with Jobs – as well as go against him. She was awarded the unofficial 'Standing up to Steve Jobs award' in 1981 and 1982.

So are you willing to stand up against everyone else, even those senior to you? And who within your organisation is prepared to stand up to you, a leader or the CEO?

VUJA DE ?

In his book *Originals*, Adam Grant discusses how as human beings our nature is to 'rationalize the status quo as legitimate.' He calls this the 'default system' and highlights the many hazards of taking the status quo for granted while never questioning the default assumptions we make.

Grant suggests flipping the old idea of déjà vu where we encounter something new, but feel like we have experienced it before to a new approach – vuja de.

Vuja de, Grant writes, 'is the reverse – we face something familiar, but we see it with a fresh perspective that enables us to gain new insight from old problems'.

Have you ever entered a meeting, training or session and prejudged the activity as wasted time before it even happened?

Next time, instead, I challenge you to enter that meeting or session with an open mind. Pay attention to three novel or unique aspects of the activity that you haven't noticed before.

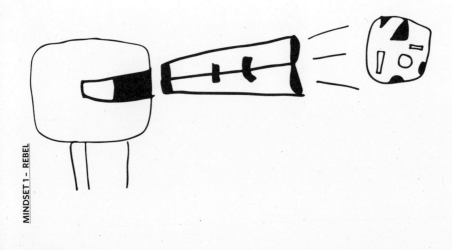

Disagree and commit

This phrase will save a lot of time. If you have conviction on a particular direction even though there's no consensus, it's helpful to say, 'Look, I know we disagree on this but will you gamble with me on it? Disagree and commit?' By the time you're at this point, no one can know the answer for sure, and you'll probably get a quick yes. This isn't one way. If you're the boss, you should do this too. I disagree and commit all the time.

This is an excerpt from a letter to Amazon shareholders from founder Jeff Bezos in April 2017. This non-conforming attitude, which filters from the top, is how the company has achieved, and continues to achieve, such enviable success. It's also why *Fast Company* named Amazon the World's Most Innovative Company in 2017.

Traditionally, senior leaders refuse to support a skunkworks project that strays outside the comfort zone. They refuse to provide the resources or support needed to succeed. In contrast, Bezos encourages disagreement and offers true support for that difference of opinion. This is a great example of a culture supporting the rebel mindset within an organisation.

Research from author Adam Grant found non-conformists who genuinely disagree with one perspective are useful even when they're wrong, because it makes us re-examine our thinking and look at challenges from different perspectives. This in turn leads to better problem identification and innovation.

This is why you must encourage constructive dissent and healthy debate with others in your organisation and in your teams, in order to push your thinking and look at problems from different angles.

A client of mine in a general manager role once told me about a scenario that happened a few years ago in his business. His CEO came to the business with an idea that he had seen successfully implemented in another market and wanted to implement it in Australia. He explained:

We didn't spend time to understand local customer needs. Everyone was frightened to tell the CEO that the numbers didn't stack up, no one challenged him. We failed to ask simple questions like, 'Why are we doing this?' or 'What customer problem does it solve?' The idea was implemented. It cost the business tens of millions of dollars and the result was that 90% of the services lost money.

DON'T BRING PEOPLE WHO THINK EXACTLY THE SAME WAY THAT YOU DO INTO CONVERSATIONS. IT PAYS TO ROCK THE BOAT.

SEARCH FOR ELEPHANTS

In a meeting recently, a client said to me, 'There is an elephant in the room that we are not allowed to talk about,' referring to a potential problem that would likely disrupt their business within the next two to five years.

The 'elephant in the room' is your most valuable problem.

The elephant is a huge opportunity for your business because if you can properly define it, solve it and tame it, it could lead you to disruptive innovation.

As a rebel, you must not only search for your organisational elephants, but also proactively pursue them as a problem to solve.

So ask yourself: What are the elephants currently hiding in your organisation?

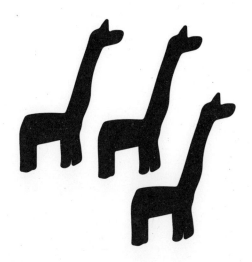

THE REBEL -FESTO

1.
Make tiny ripples or big waves

3.
Don't blend in, stand out

2.
Be willing to ruin a party

4.
Fear the mundane

5.
**Challenge
the status quo**

8.
**Live outside your
comfort zone**

6.
Break the rules

9.
**Lead the way, everyone is on a
different path to you**

7.
**Befriend the
dissidents**

10.
**Don't give a f*ck about what
anyone else thinks**

You can have a rebel mindset, even if you don't aspire to start a revolution. All it requires is that you follow these 10 points.

We need to encourage a rebel mindset to unlock possibilities and breakthrough thinking. It requires a new playbook, one where:

Curiosity and problem finding is a not a one-off activity, it is a continuous part of the business culture.

Leaders are willing to leave the zone of comfort and step into the zone of possibilities.

Cognitive diversity and non-conformity is emphasised for breakthrough thinking.

Dissidents are encouraged to think differently and to challenge authority and the status quo.

As the rebel Steve Jobs once said:

Here's to the crazy ones, the misfits, the rebels, the troublemakers, the round pegs in the square holes ... the ones who see things differently – they're not fond of rules ... You can quote them, disagree with them, glorify or vilify them, but the only thing you can't do is ignore them because they change things ... they push the human race forward, and while some may see them as the crazy ones, we see genius, because the ones who are crazy enough to think that they can change the world, are the ones who do.

So are you ready and confident to be an outlier and stand out in your business?

ARE YOU A REBEL ?

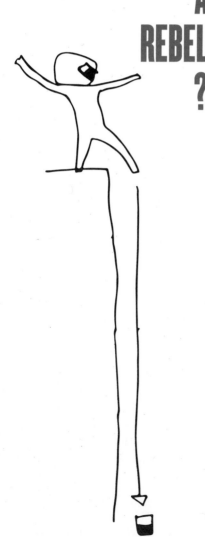

Do you state what you believe to be true without fear of consequences?

Do you look for ways to do things differently?

Are you prepared to go against the grain and question your own authority?

Are you prepared to take calculated risks?

Are you willing to give yourself and others permission to experiment and grow?

Do you search out the elephants in the room?

MINDSET 2
ZEN-MASTER

'If your mind is empty,

it is always ready for anything; it is open to everything.'

Shunryu Suzuki

The Sydney 2000 Olympic Games marked the 100th anniversary of the admission of women to the Olympics. Indigenous Australian Cathy Freeman was given the honour of carrying the Olympic torch and lighting the cauldron. She was the most talked about Australian competitor in the lead up to the event. Her two world championship titles in 1997 and 1999 had cemented her as firm race favourite. Furthermore, she was seen by many Australians as a symbol of reconciliation – black and white united in pride and spirit.

Can you imagine the pressure Cathy felt as she entered the stadium?

On September 25, she stepped onto the track at Sydney Olympic Park in her iconic green, yellow and silver bodysuit, which paid tribute to her country, and her red, black and yellow running spikes honouring her Aboriginal heritage. As each of the athletes were announced at the start line, a deafening roar greeted Cathy's name.

'I was like a lamb walking into the lion's den,' said Cathy when I interviewed her about this moment. 'I didn't want to get caught up in all of the chaos of the race. I knew if I did, I may have gone out too hard and then I would've stuffed it.'

So rather than get distracted she, '... fell into a trance. The words that came into my mind were: "Just do what you know." It was like this peace came over me,' she said.

'I can't even remember the noise. I tuned into my body, and that's how I tuned out. It's a strange sensation. That's being fully present.'

In the last 100 metres of the race, Freeman powered past her opponents and crossed the finish line in first place, way ahead of her closest rivals.

'In that split moment, as I was mid-air over the finish line, it was the first moment I had the chance to feel like I could let go,' she said. 'I only remember the noise after I crossed the line. The light switch went on, and it was like "where am I?" It's almost like I came out of a deep sleep, woke up from a dream and found myself in this place where they're carrying on like crazy. I felt totally disorientated, and I had to sit down, just to get some stability under my body.'

If you watched the race, it is a moment in history you will never forget. But the real power lies in Cathy's description of how she *felt* before, during and after the race. Of what she was *thinking* when she 'tuned in to tune out' and win.

What Cathy describes is a zen-master mindset.

Get zen

The zen-master is an expert at clearing their mind to create a blank slate, and become open to new knowledge and experiences. They allow themselves to get into a state where everything else disappears – all the monkey mind, internal chatter and distractions – so that things flow effortlessly.

Psychologist Mihaly Csikszentmihalyi defines flow as an 'optimal state of consciousness where we feel our best and perform our best.' Flow is more than just inhabiting the here and now, it's about a higher level of functioning.

IT IS THIS PEAK PERFORMANCE THAT WE NEED TO FIND OUR MOST VALUABLE PROBLEMS.

Finding problems, using our curiosity, doesn't happen by following a recipe, it is not a linear or rapid process. Most of the time tapping into our curiosity just happens naturally and sporadically. So we need to be awake to what is happening around us with our customers, clients and everyday experiences through listening and observation.

WHEN YOU HAVE A ZEN-MASTER MINDSET, YOU ARE OPEN AND RECEPTIVE TO CURIOUS MOMENTS, TO FINDING OPPORTUNITIES, MAKING DISCOVERIES, AND ADDING MEANING TO YOUR INSIGHTS AND OBSERVATIONS.

Finding clues to the right problem to solve can take time to uncover. It is not something you can rush, so you need to be patient and be in the moment for when the key insights reveal themselves to you.

WHEN IT ALL GOES PEAR SHAPED

Athletes like Cathy Freeman train hard, committing their entire life to the mastery of their discipline so that when they stand on the start line, they are confident they have done all the work they can possibly do to be ready. This kind of dedication and focus takes time and practice.

In my interview with Cathy, she also reflected on a time at the 1995 World Championships in Gothenburg when she was anything but zen.

'I remember in the race thinking – but you don't have thoughts in your head when you're in the zone. Things went totally pear-shaped and I went out far too hard and felt it slipping away. I went from first, second, third and then fourth, it was awful.'

What went wrong?

'I was totally obsessed with the notion of winning, I spent every single second of my day, even on the toilet, head in my hands, just running it over and over in my head. I got anxious and uptight.'

She had become focused on the outcome, of winning, instead of on the process.

Think about how often you get caught up on the outcome or a solution, rather than spending the time being curious about the journey you're about to head on. Now what would happen if you stopped and paid attention to what is happening in the present instead? Would you find better problems to solve?

Productivity problems

In organisations we are mostly time poor. We spend our day hopping from one meeting to the next, never really doing exactly what we set out to do. So as a result, we multi-task.

We try to save time by doing multiple things at once, switching from one task to another, or performing tasks in rapid succession. But the reality is that we are actually wasting time. Research shows that multi-tasking, even brief mental blocks created by shifting between tasks can reduce productivity by 40%.

Even minor distractions can have an overwhelming effect. One workplace study found we have on average almost 87 interruptions per day (some external interruptions and some triggered by ourselves). Getting back on task following an interruption took, an average of 23 minutes, and 18% of the time the interrupted task was not resumed that same day.

Our brains are not designed for multi-tasking. This is actually called 'task switching'. If you're physically present in a meeting and switch tasks to check your email, you are no longer engaged in the content of the session. You can only conduct one cognitive activity at a time. So you can talk or listen, you can read or type, you can listen or read.

Shifting your attention from one task to another disrupts your concentration and destroys your focus. Each time you return to the initial task you use valuable cognitive resources and time reorienting yourself.

IF YOU'RE MULTI-TASKING YOU WILL MISS VALUABLE PROBLEMS AND INSIGHTS.

If we are so busy multi-tasking or thinking about things that aren't related to the job at hand, how can we possibly have room for anything new, for curiosity, let alone finding valuable problems to solve?

If your head is full of irrelevant 'stuff', then you won't have the energy or space to be open to new thinking, for innovating, for finding and solving your most valuable problem.

We live in a fast-paced world of work, where we have lots of competing priorities. The average person is estimated to have between 50,000 and 70,000 thoughts per day, and research has found that we spend about 47% of our waking hours thinking about something other than what we are actually doing.

A zen-master shuts out this noise and focuses on finding the most valuable problem to solve. And I guarantee, they are not distracted by emails.

BECOME A BETTER PROBLEM FINDER

Be deliberately present
Stay aware and awake to what is going on around you and what is going on within you. Give your full attention to seemingly mundane tasks like the feel and texture of a door handle you touch to open.

Become a single-tasker
Focus on the task at hand, not several all at once. Switch off as many distractions as you can, including notifications on your devices.

Tune
out to tune in
Practise a moment of stillness. Pause for several minutes to tune in and notice your breath, focus on just the one thing – your body is breathing. Slow down to speed up your day.

Challenge
yourself to be present
Refrain from checking your phone or thinking about your next meeting or what you will have for lunch. If you catch yourself thinking about these things, acknowledge that the thought has occurred without dwelling on it, then return your focus to the task at hand.

Is it a game of darts you're playing?

In an innovation project I worked on recently, the team had been given a challenge by a senior leader of the business, which was to deliver a significant innovation in market within 12 months.

The team got immediately caught up in the solution they needed to create. They were focused on the outcome rather than spending time in the present moment to focus on being curious and identifying the right problem to solve.

So, instead of asking each member of the team to first gather facts about the situation and find the most valuable problem to solve, they were instructed to go out and find solutions. Each of them filled in the blanks differently, and as a result, started running in different directions. This approach is like gathering darts without working out first whether darts is even the game you are going to play.

When we don't spend time in the present to learn about the here and now, we are likely to jump to conclusions, to jump to solving problems too quickly – which as you already know is one of the issues facing organisations today.

By contrast, when we have a zen-master mindset, we are open to expanding ourselves and learning. We learn to block out distractions. We have a deep concentration and focus for a challenge, and we tune in to the present to help us identify customer problems worthy of solving.

Being zen helps us to create wonder and excitement from the mundane, and to value the process of problem finding and understanding the right problems to solve. It is only by adopting a zen-master mindset that we learn the discipline of practising curiosity and problem finding.

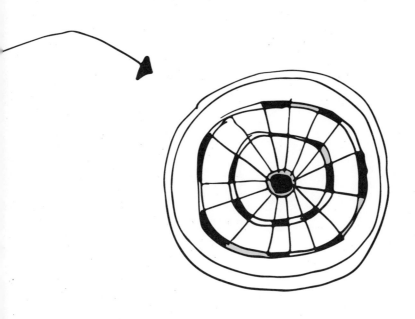

ARE YOU PAYING ATTENTION ?

Try the following exercise with at least two people as a way to bring your mind to the present moment before a big day of work.

Get people into pairs and ask them to identify one partner as A and the other as B.

Ask partner B to close their eyes, then tell them that partner A has 60 seconds to change three things about themselves. For example, they might take off their glasses, tie up their hair, take off or put on a jacket, put a pen in their pocket.

Now, ask Partner B to open their eyes and see if they can identify the three things that Partner A changed. Give them 60 seconds. Once time is up, congratulate everyone.

You can repeat the exercise, swapping roles, so each person gets a turn at changing and noticing.

The most important part of this activity is in the debrief.

Ask people:

What happened?

How did you go the second time you were given the same instructions? What changed for you? What did you learn?

How can you make noticing the little things a practice in your everyday work?

ARE YOU A ZEN-MASTER?

Do you have energy available for curiosity and new thinking?

Are you present and tuned in to the current moment?

Do you devote time to thinking, not just doing?

Are you open to learning something new about yourself, your customers or your business?

Are you able to block out unnecessary distractions?

Are you a single-tasker?

MINDSET 3
NOVICE

'In the beginner's mind

there are many possibilities, but in the expert's mind there are few.'

Shunryu Suzuki

I want you to draw a bike in your mind (yes, really). Just a simple everyday pushbike that you've probably seen and used thousands of times.

The instructions below are taken from an actual study by cognitive psychologist Dr. Rebecca Lawson:

It does not matter if your lines are wobbly or whatever. What I am interested in is what you know about how bicycles work. I want to make you think about what the pedals of the bike do ... and what the chain of the bike does ... and why the frame of the bike is a particular shape ... and how you steer a bike. So I want you to think about how a bike works before you draw in the parts.

Participants in this study actually viewed pictures with four different arrangements of chains, pedals and frames, and were then asked which option corresponded to the usual position in a working bicycle.

The result? Over 40% of them couldn't pick the standard arrangement. Some even believed that the chain went around the front wheel, as well as the back one.

Most people's understanding of this familiar, everyday object was sketchy and shallow, even though it was frequently encountered and easily perceived.

This is referred to in psychology as the Illusion of Explanatory Depth (IOED), which means we think we understand familiar phenomena far better than we actually do.

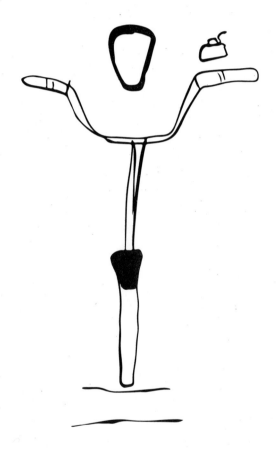

YOU PROBABLY DON'T KNOW AS MUCH AS YOU THINK YOU DO ABOUT YOUR BUSINESS, YOUR CUSTOMERS, YOUR OPERATIONS, OR YOUR COMPETITORS.

Most of us think we have all the answers, even when it comes to familiar things, but when pressed on the spot to draw or describe something, we struggle to find the right words or pictures.

Discovering gaps in our knowledge and understanding is important for innovation – no matter how big or small those gaps are.

Know it all?

As leaders within organisations we are encouraged to be the expert, to know it all, to know what is best. After all, you're in charge so you know best, right?

There is a misconception that if you don't know everything about something in your organisation then you shouldn't really be the leader. But this couldn't be further from the truth.

Doing something for a very long time, or being promoted into senior management roles might make someone feel entitled or obligated to be the expert and have strong opinions. We tend to believe that our value is directly tied to our performance to do something well and we often avoid doing things we can't do well that might make us look bad.

Even if we don't feel like an expert, then at the very least we are encouraged to 'fake it until we make it' to convey that we know what's going on. Conveying the mindset of an expert gives us credibility within organisations, but it can come at a cost.

Being an expert makes you ~~blind~~ to finding problems.

You're more likely to jump to conclusions and misunderstand the problem, or potentially solve the wrong problem, which then turns into a complete waste of time, money and resources. After all, it doesn't matter how good your solution is if you are solving the wrong problem.

ARE YOU AN EXPERT ?

You make up your mind quickly even if you don't have all the facts.

You spend more of your day providing answers than asking questions.

You are expected to know things, people in your organisation come to you for answers or your opinion.

You might not know everything, but you are not willing to admit that.

You don't have time to waste exploring unfamiliar territories, you need facts and evidence to support what you are trying to do.

If you agree with most of these statements, then your expert mindset is potentially closing you off to possibilities.

Flip your thinking

In an experiment conducted by social psychologist Dr. Victor Ottati, participants who had equal levels of a domain knowledge were manipulated into perceiving themselves as 'experts' (i.e. relatively knowledgeable in a domain) or 'novices' (possessing a limited amount of knowledge).

The participants who were induced to feel like experts tended to respond to a follow-up questionnaire in a more closed-minded manner, while those who were made to feel like novices responded in a more open-minded manner.

This suggests that if you think you are an expert – or think you should convey yourself to be the expert – you are more likely to be closed-minded and less curious. By contrast, if you look at the world with a child-like beginner's mind and shift your self-perception to that of a novice, you will be more open-minded to valuable problems to solve and better ways of doing things. Like the way we discovered in RECOGNISE – NOT REWARD.

The differences can be summarised simply, as shown in Figure 5.1.

The expert	The novice
Judges	Defers judgment
Answers questions	Asks questions
Is ego-driven	Shows humility
Is guarded	Is open
Seeks the known	Seeks the unknown

Figure 5.1: Expert versus novice

Embracing a novice mindset involves being vulnerable, being willing to admit that you might not have all of the answers. You'll allow yourself to stay in question mode, to cast the net wide to discover new knowledge and insights, and you pause before jumping to conclusions.

To be a novice is to deliberately hunt for customer problems and pain points that require solving.

Consequently, customer problems will be more fully understood and defined. Meaning that your organisation can better articulate the problems you are trying to solve, which will ultimately lead to better solutions.

Catriona Larritt, Chief Commercial Officer at Jetstar Airways, demonstrates this beautifully when discussing her 30-year-old digital mentor:

Part of being curious is being humble enough to know that you don't know everything. So I mentor a woman in the team from a career point of view, and she mentors me from a digital point of view. I'll even ask silly questions like 'How do you think about curating content on Instagram?' Or, 'How is Google evolving and thinking about Micro-Moments?' We're always individually learning, and helping to create a learning organisation.

BEGINNER'S MIND

Zen Buddhism teaches the concept of 'beginner's mind', Shoshin, as a positive attribute, something to cultivate.

A beginner's mind is open and aware, alert to new information and experiences. When we cultivate this mindset, we free ourselves from expectation. We are invited to explore the world unburdened by past experiences and previous knowledge.

In the beginner's mind there are multiple possibilities. It refers to having an attitude of openness, eagerness, and lack of preconceptions when studying a subject, even when studying at an advanced level. Just as a beginner in that subject would.

Imagine you are a child again, trying to learn to ride a bike for the first time. What are all the different elements you need to think about to stay upright and move forwards? Holding the handle bars, pedalling, balancing the bike etc. We take riding a bike for granted now, because we are the expert and we don't even think about the detail of what is needed to ride a bike. (Most of us can't even accurately describe or draw all of the parts of a bike, as demonstrated at the start of this chapter).

How might your work be different if you approached it without expectations and assumptions, without knowing anything at all? How might you go back to the beginning of how something works, or why your customers do things the way they do?

Unlearning the learning

Try this quick exercise with a couple of friends or colleagues.

Ask them to stand up. Tell them you are going to give them instructions on which direction to look in. They have to turn their head (only their head) and look in the appropriate direction. Up, down, left or right.

Say the words up, down, left, and right in a random order and encourage them to follow your instructions. Keep giving directions at a fairly rapid pace.

After about a minute, tell them that you are going to make a change. From now on, up will mean down and vice versa. So when you say down, they should look up at the ceiling. Similarly, when you say up, they should look down at their feet.

Explain that the meaning of the words 'left' and 'right' remain the same. Call out the four directions in a random order and ask them to follow these instructions. Remind them, that they have to remember the new meaning of the words 'up' and 'down'.

You will no doubt see many 'mistakes' and hear lots of embarrassed laughter. You can probably imagine just by reading the above.

This simple exercise shows how it takes a lot of practice and discipline to unlearn what we have learned.

There is often an uncomfortable feeling of vulnerability, especially as a leader, to be the novice. It requires you to cross the threshold of the known into the unknown. It requires your willingness to go back and to be not so good at new things again. To have to go back to being a beginner in order to acquire new knowledge, can be scary, embarrassing and frustrating.

After interviewing numerous executives, I have learned that they feel most comfortable in the role of the novice when their job role changes or they move on to a new company. This is where they find themselves on the steepest learning curve and where they feel it's okay putting their hand in the air to say, 'Hey I don't know everything, let's start at the beginning.'

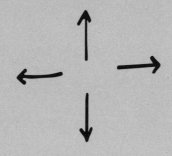

If you think you know everything then you are never going to

LEARN.

Inevitably, whether it's through culture, experience or routine, everyone will eventually become an expert.

How many times have you heard the reference to, it takes 10,000 hours to have mastery of something, i.e. to become an expert? I have done my 10,000 hours in customer interviewing, observation and facilitation to be able to call myself an expert. However, my continued success in the work I do is through having a novice mindset day in and day out. It is about knowing and understanding the benefits of being a novice and embodying this novice mindset into the all of the work I do.

The same applies to you.

EXPERT BEES

I learned this game from Gert Garman, who for many years was a creative problem solver at The Walt Disney Company in the USA. Try this in a group setting where you have at least six people.

First begin by asking everyone to get into pairs. Ask the tallest person in each pair to assume the role of the expert. The expert is world renowned, and whatever they say can't be wrong.

The shortest person in each pair is the novice. Their role is to ask the expert questions. They can ask anything at all, and the expert will always know the answer.

Tell the expert to assume their job role involves providing therapy to bees. Begin play by asking the novice to ask the expert questions about this role.

After several minutes of questions and answers, ask the players to stop and swap roles – the expert becomes the novice and the novice the expert. The new expert is a coach who trains elephants to parachute out of airplanes.

Allow another few minutes for questions and answers.

The playfulness of this activity completely changes the energy of the room. There are no wrong or right answers and the possibilities generated are endless. I've heard everything from managing politics in the beehive to bees with flower phobias.

Tellingly, people always seem to find it easier to be the expert than the novice. Assuming the role of the novice is something that takes practice and attention to master. It can be easy to unwittingly slip back into the expert mindset.

Sound silly?

Have your ever been in a meeting where someone has asked you, 'Do you know much about concept X?' and even though you don't really know much about it you reply 'Yes'.

You portrayed yourself as an expert and in doing so you didn't learn anything further. You never got to understand the meaning behind the conversation. Perhaps you went away after the meeting and Googled it, but you never got to understand the context or intention around the concept. You let your ego get in the way of your curiosity.

This happens every single day via the use of buzz words. Though we often use buzz words, their meaning can mean different things to different people. They often mask a gap in our knowledge, serving as placeholders that gloss over concepts we don't fully understand.

What it really comes down to is not wanting to look silly in front of our team, peers or boss. So what if we were to reframe 'silly' questions into 'clarifying' questions?

We would create a new frame of questioning that doesn't threaten our ego and provides a tool to unlock deep knowledge and understanding.

The added benefit of asking clarifying questions is that there is a chance other people will also learn something from it, and they may even ask a question that they were not previously game to ask.

I was facilitating a client workshop recently and asked a clarifying question. This led to a realisation that more than a quarter of the room were not sure if the organisation they worked at was privately or government owned.

ASK YOURSELF:

do you create a culture where people feel like there's no repercussion or humiliation for asking clarifying questions?

To embrace your child-like curiosity, perhaps in your next meeting you could start with some of the following statements:

Pretend that I know nothing about this topic ...

Explain this to me like you are explaining it to your grandmother ...

Let's go right back to the start, as we might be missing something, and assume I am a first-time user ...

How can you look at everyday experiences more deeply? How can you look for the unfamiliar within the familiar?

When you learn to be a novice by embracing the unknown and learning to ask 'silly' questions, you can uncover great insights you are not expecting. Innovation comes from uncovering the right question, not the answer. So it's about finding the right question to ask.

Learning to embrace the unknown and question the obvious and familiar can open up new thinking and possibilities in amazing and surprising ways.

LUV A SILLY QUESTION

Curiosity has remained with me as a management tool as much as it is a philosophy for finding problems.

I have learnt to suspend judgment, to slow down, rather than jump to solve a problem too fast. Remaining curious means you keep asking clarifying questions in order for everyone to get grounded in the same place as you, so you move to a solution together.

When the building is on fire, it's okay to jump ahead, and make rapid decisions for other people. But most of the time, businesses aren't on fire and there isn't a disaster and you have got some time to ask curious questions.

I think it's a matter of checking yourself and saying, 'Am I sure I know everything? But more importantly, do I have time to go back and just learn a few more opinions?'

When you're curious, you say, 'Okay, that might be it, you're right. But what else might it be?' And you continue to explore it. This way, you'll actually generate potential opportunities, which you then get curious about and explore further. You might find that some of them contributed to the problem in some way.

Being a CEO gives me the freedom to ask silly questions.

When I drive out to where the duck farms are, I often describe myself as swimming in the very shallow end of the pool of knowledge. By default, I become curious.

I say to my employees, 'I know you all might know the answer to this, but can you tell me why we do this?' Eight out of ten times, people will answer very quickly, and then every now and then, they'll go, 'You know, I'm not sure why we do it that way. That's a good question.'

So the curiosity is raised within that person to understand why we do it. Sometimes it's historical and it's correct, other times it's just always the way we've done it, so there might be a better way.

Part of the problem of asking the silly question is the fear of being embarrassed. I think most people will have experienced that, but as the CEO that's relatively new, I have no fear of that.

I often think that the culture of a business is the worst standard the most senior person will accept. If you accept as the CEO that it's okay to ask clarifying

questions, you have a culture that accepts it's okay, (I like to call it clarifying questions because it sounds better than stupid questions), then other people are more likely to learn something out of asking that question. But there's also a chance other people will learn out of hearing the answer, for a question they may not have been game to ask.

So create a safe environment where people feel like there's no repercussions or humiliation for asking a question. Some often turn out to be quite insightful questions.

Daryl Bussell, CEO, Luv-à-Duck

Never assume

The novice is always looking for new people or things to learn from. They are seeking better ways to do things, they are hunting for new problems to solve. The novice is confident saying 'I don't know' or 'why do we do things this way?' The novice never assumes they know the answer to anything.

Adopting a novice mindset will open your mind to observing and learning, and ultimately will lead you to new possibilities that you may have never imagined. You and your business will benefit from this mindset, where customer problems will be more fully understood. This will ultimately lead to better innovation.

CEO and Founder Uday Dandavate finds one of Buddha's quotes particularly useful to live by:

Do not believe in anything (simply) because you have heard it; Do not believe in traditions, because they been handed down for many generations; Do not believe in anything, because it is spoken and rumored by many; Do not believe in anything simply because it is found written in your religious books; But after observation and analysis, when you find that anything agrees with reason and is conducive to the good and benefit of one and all, then accept it and live up to it.

Check your ego

Think of a topic you are really passionate and knowledgeable about. Something you might contemplate doing a TedTalk on. Now imagine you find yourself at a conference on this topic.

You sit down next to a stranger who strikes up a conversation about this topic that you know so well. They seem really interested in what you know, and so you take advantage of the opportunity to tell them everything you can. They listen respectfully, taking everything in and even making careful notes.

It's time for the next speaker at the conference. You have really been looking forward to this session. This is someone you have read so much about. You would go as far as to say they are the guru on this topic. As the speaker is introduced, to your surprise, the person you have been talking to stands up and makes their way to the podium.

You kick yourself. How does that make you feel? Has your lack of curiosity resulted in you missing out on the opportunity to learn something new?

Your ego is the image you have of yourself and the social mask you put on for the world.

Have you ever heard yourself saying the following secretly to yourself?

I'm not going to learn anything I don't already know.

I've seen it all before.

This is my job; I already know what I need to do.

Stop wasting time, let's just get on with it.

Customers don't know what they want, that's what I am here for.

As improv actor Mike McEvoy explains, 'The moment you're trying to be clever, or you overthink things, is the moment that your own ego takes over'.

Your ego can get in the way of your curiosity, and impact on decisions you make, but only if you let it. Humility is an important aspect to this. The act of allowing yourself to be open to not knowing everything, elicits your curiosity to explore, question and discover. This in turn makes you feel good, and helps you to learn and identify valuable problems.

CHECK YOURSELF

Jon arrived at a consumer co-creation session I was facilitating accompanied by attitude and lots of negative body language (i.e. crossed arms and a look of boredom). At times, throughout the session, he would pull aside other colleagues to have side conversations. His body language displayed a general lack of interest and his lack of note-taking spoke volumes.

In contrast, from the moment Joe walked into a session I was running at a different organisation, he smiled, he nodded and he showed customers he was interested. He paid close attention to what they created, what energised them, what they struggled with. He asked them questions, respectfully listened and took copious notes that would rival a professional note-taker.

Who do you think was more curious and benefited from the insights that emerged in these consumer sessions?

We can get caught up in thinking we know what our customers want, make huge assumptions about what they think or how they feel, or perhaps how they will use our product or service.

Sometimes you might think you have all the answers, or even that part of the answer is good enough to start coming up with solutions, but this actually puts a stop to your curiosity before it even begins.

As artist Cameron Hayes puts it, 'To be curious, you have to stay ignorant. You have to say that I'm glad that I don't know stuff. I'm comfortable not knowing.'

ARE YOU A NOVICE ?

Are you prepared to ask seemingly silly questions?

Do you create a culture where there are no repercussions for asking silly questions?

Do you focus on questions and not worry about being the expert with all the answers?

Are you willing to show some vulnerability?

Are you comfortable when you don't have all the answers?

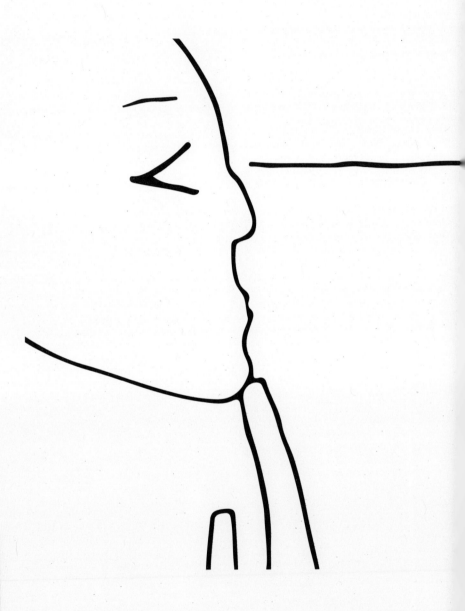

MINDSET 4
SLEUTH

'Never theorise before you have data.

Invariably you end up twisting the facts to suit theories instead of theories to suit facts.'

Sherlock Holmes

Barry Marshall was a curious medical resident at the Fremantle Hospital in Perth, Western Australia. He was so hell-bent on trying to define the root cause of a patient problem – peptic ulcers, which are extremely painful and a significant risk for stomach cancer – that he decided to experiment on himself.

Ulcers were seen as the result of people living unhealthy lifestyles. No one in the medical community believed bacteria could live in the stomach. It was believed there was too much acid for bacteria to exist.

'I was so frustrated,' says Marshall in the *Medical Journal of Australia*. 'I really needed to prove this organism could infect a healthy human stomach. So I decided to put my money where my mouth was.'

Marshall walked over to the lab bench, drank a petri dish cultured with Helicobacter pylori bacteria, and in days became quite unwell and within weeks had proved that this bacteria had colonised in his stomach.

'I suspect I was born with a boundless curiosity and this was encouraged through my childhood,' says Marshall of his discovery. It's this curiosity that led him to being awarded the Nobel prize in 2005.

Marshall was a sleuth, he had lots of clues that were helping him to define his patients' problem. He had listened to what others were saying and had spent decades looking at the evidence and research.

It wasn't until he experienced the problem himself that he was able to obtain the final clue he needed to convince the medical community of their most valuable problem.

As Marshall himself explains:

The best kind of research is curiosity-driven research. It could lead to something ... you don't know where it is going to end up when you make small new discoveries.

Look beyond the obvious

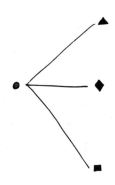

Curiosity is about seeking clues and inspiration from everyday interactions to observe the little things. It requires your attention. Problem finding requires deliberate observation.

In general, we understand 'observe' is 'to notice or perceive something, and register it as being significant.' Whereas when you 'look' at something you are more likely to 'gaze in a specified direction'.

Too often we look at things without really observing what is really happening and why this might be. It's a subtle, yet very powerful distinction.

Yet looking is what organisations do every day.

ORGANISATIONS JUMP TOO QUICKLY INTO SOLVING

what they perceive their customers' problems to be, based on what customers have told them, instead of observing what the real issue is.

You can't just rely on what you hear from behind the glass of a focus group, second-hand sound bites from colleagues or your own personal interactions and experiences.

Your life and experiences are not the same as everyone else's life and experiences. Careful observation is therefore an imperative.

We find our most valuable problems to solve by spending time with customers discovering their hopes, fears and values, and viewing the world through their eyes. Noticing what delights them and observing their irritations, frustrations and pain points.

YOU NEED TO CURIOUSLY OBSERVE WHAT PEOPLE SAY, AND WHAT THEY DO, SO YOU CAN UNDERSTAND WHAT MATTERS TO THEM.

Your world and your customers' worlds are made up of countless tiny, almost unnoticeable moments each day that provide you with the clues to valuable problems that need solving. For example:

Why is that person checking the crispiness of their samosa the moment they open the box?

Why are there so many unfinished bottles of iced tea in a food court?

Why does that lady put on gloves to put petrol into her car?

Why is that person walking around the house in a t-shirt and shorts in the middle of winter, with the temperature set at 25 degrees?

It's the really little things we notice that can lead us to the greatest insights.

Seeing with new eyes
Subtle insights can pass you quickly if you are not primed to notice them. Blink and you will miss them. As French novelist Marcel Proust said, 'The real act of discovery consists not in finding new lands but in seeing with new eyes.'

Think about two identically designed university dorm rooms. Vacant, they look identical, but fast forward a few weeks into semester and individual occupants have left their mark on the physical environment. Think about your own bedroom and office. What does it convey about you and your personality?

Psychologist Samuel Gosling had a hypothesis that the physical environment that people craft around themselves is rich with information about their personality, ability, value and lifestyles. To test his theory, he and his colleagues asked people to step into the office and bedrooms of strangers and then rate their personality using the Big Five personality trait measures. They weren't given any background or context about strangers they were evaluating (photos and names were hidden). They had to rely entirely on cues such as personal items, decorating style, level of organisation.

People were incredibly accurate in their personality assessments. Gosling demonstrated that everyday people who step in the home of a stranger can accurately predict the stranger's personality.

What this tells us is that through contextual observation and stepping into the shoes of your customers, you can gain incredible clues that lead to a deeper understanding of their needs, values and pain points.

HOW'S YOUR STEAK?

Has this ever happened to you? You're at a restaurant and there's something wrong with your meal. Maybe your steak is overcooked, your vegetables are squishy, or you find a piece of hair in your food. You complain to your dinner companion about it, but when the restaurant manager asks you, 'How was your meal?' you reply, 'It was great, thanks.'

Now imagine you are the restaurant manager. If you relied on this single piece of feedback 'It was great' then the interaction would stop, there. You'd think that there was no problem to solve. However, if you noticed that the meal was unfinished and observed the person's body language – perhaps they had their arms crossed or avoided eye contact – and you paid attention to the tone of the response, you would no doubt pick up that something was wrong.

Perhaps you even go one step further and order the same meal yourself to truly step into their shoes, and experience the meal. Observing is more than just seeing with your eyes – it is looking, listening and experiencing.

Relying on information from one input is like trying to solve a jigsaw puzzle with only 25% of the pieces.

Insights are a collection of clues which, when gathered together, tell the story of your data. You need to use the sleuth mindset to seek clues and inspiration from everyday interactions through this kind of observation.

What people say, ain't necessarily what they do

Lilah was a 64-year-old retired teacher who had survived two bouts of cancer. She lived in Florida with her second husband in a trailer park. Between them they had seven children and three grandchildren.

Lilah loved to bake and cook and keep busy doing crafts (sometimes she had the motivation to get up and work on her miniature doll houses at two or three in the morning). She was something of an entrepreneur, with an online arts and crafts business that she ran from one of the bedrooms, that she'd converted into a work studio. The business had given her a sense of purpose and identity.

When I stepped inside her home I noticed framed family photographs adorning the living area, which I soon learned were important to her. She talked to each of her kids every Sunday, calling them to see how they were going. She also enjoyed receiving emails with photos of her grandchildren.

She described technology as a lifeline for her. She used it not just for her business, but also to communicate with her family, who didn't live in Florida. She especially loved her landline telephone because she said she could hear and feel the emotion in people's voices.

However, Lilah didn't use the telephone as often as she would have liked to, because she was very cost-conscious. She had a monthly set income and needed to manage her budget, so she bought phone cards and used email instead.

I asked Lilah to show me her computer, her favourite webpages she had bookmarked (e.g. an airline where she had purchased tickets, various craft supply sites, and her own arts and crafts site), as well as how she managed business orders. For the next 20 minutes, I watched her struggle to turn on her computer, patiently connect to dial-up internet and wait an eternity for her business webpage to load. When it finally popped up, it was difficult to navigate and although Lilah was familiar with the site, she lost her place several times, and had to refresh or return to the homepage.

Yet she never once complained about this painful interaction.

Lilah commented that her provider had offered to upgrade her connection to DSL internet. However, she had declined as she didn't really understand what that meant. 'I am always home, I don't really need all the fastness,' were her exact words.

Lilah did not own a mobile phone and was contemplating buying one. She was about to embark on a road trip to Wisconsin with her husband and she felt they might need one in case of an emergency. She said she wanted a bigger phone, as she thought it would be easier to talk.

If she had been in a focus group, then in the few minutes we interacted I would only have learned, that Lilah loves her family, runs an online business, books airline tickets online, buys her arts and craft supplies online, has two favourite communication tools (her computer and landline), and wants to buy a mobile phone for an upcoming trip. However, by being in Lilah's home, I actually got to observe how she used each of the different technology tools.

WHAT PEOPLE SAY, AND WHAT THEY DO

ARE TWO VERY, VERY DIFFERENT THINGS.

I was working for a global mobile phone manufacturer at the time of this field visit. The company was looking to understand the needs and pain points of older consumers.

So we could say that some of the clues that I observed from Lilah were:

Lilah's access to technology had empowered her and given her confidence, it had given her a purpose and was tied to her identity.

She didn't understand what DSL internet was and didn't know better alternatives to her current experience existed.

The landline phone was on the highest ringtone and piercingly loud to an observer – yet she had difficulty hearing it.

The landline phone had extremely large protruding buttons, but she often had trouble dialling the correct numbers.

Lilah was nervous about travelling in the car without a mobile phone – it made her feel vulnerable.

Lilah had a limited disposable income to spend on any additional internet and communication tools.

These clues around Lilah's needs, wants and problems became product opportunities for my client to solve for older consumers. The problem statement was: How might we develop a device that allows Lilah to hear and see the people she wants to communicate with?

People like Lilah are often not aware of problems and are pretty happy with the status quo. Many of the problems I discovered in this brief interaction were not articulated. I noticed them through observation.

It is a classic example of how what people say and what they do are very different.

Step into their shoes

It is not always practical to spend time in people's homes or shadow them on a customer experience, but you can still gather clues using empathy to personally step through a customer experience.

For example, several years ago, Coles Supermarkets launched its $150 basket shop. John Durkan Managing Director of Coles gave senior management the ultimate challenge: to buy a week's worth of groceries for $150. (That's how much a low-income family has to spend at the supermarket according to the Australian Bureau of Statistics Household Expenditure Survey.)

Natalie Mitchell, Research Manager at Coles, explained how the research program worked:

We would explain that you've got a family of four, with two teenage kids, and we need you to go buy six dinners, school lunches, and assume everything is in the pantry so you don't have to go buy salt and pepper and flour. You've got to buy a toothbrush, you're out of shampoo, you're out of toothpaste; and a couple other items like that. And your kids are having an Xbox party this week. Executives would then be given a 45-minute time limit in which to complete their task, to replicate the shopping experience of busy mums and dads.

Reports back from the experience included comments like 'frustrating' because multi-buy specials 'forced me to buy more to get a good price'. While others lamented the challenge of 'trying to buy healthy, fresh options and watching the price of fresh produce eat away at my budget.'

In the background, the Coles research team invited mums to critique the executive trolleys and give them scores.

Natalie explained:

There were some executives who would buy two litres of milk for the week and a mum would say, 'How is that going to feed two teenage sons? You can't have two apples, we needed 20.' It was a real eye opener.

BEWARE THE INVISIBLE GORILLA

Psychologists have long known that selective attention (concentrating closely on one particular thing) affects the way you perceive the world around you. I love the example of the 'invisible gorilla' that demonstrates this brilliantly.

Psychologists Dr. Daniel Simons and Dr. Christopher Chabris asked participants in a study to watch a video in which a group of people pass a basketball to one another. They asked them to count how many times the people in white tossed the ball. (If you haven't already seen it, Google 'invisible gorilla'.)

In the middle of the video, a person in a gorilla suit walks into the frame while the people in white continue to pass the basketball to one another. You'd think that's a pretty obvious interruption, yet it was only noticed by about half of the participants.

It wasn't that the participants weren't paying attention, but their selective attention had caused inattentional blindness. Inattentional blindness is the failure to notice a fully visible but unexpected object or event when you are focusing your attention on something else. When you are so focused on counting the ball passes or spotting a gorilla, you can miss other unexpected clues or facts.

What this highlights is that we can be blind to seemingly obvious facts, and we can be blind to our own blindness. When you are searching for facts you need to be careful of focusing too closely on hypotheses or assumptions, as this may cause you to miss unexpected clues.

You need to cast your problem finding net as wide as possible and keep your eyes wide open.

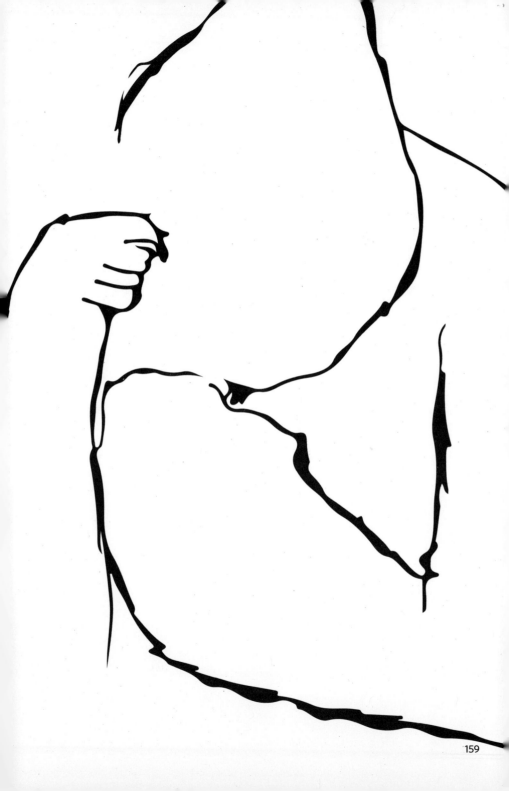

Empty your mind

We are programmed from birth to make cognitive shortcuts. These shortcuts help us make quick decisions, but are not guaranteed to always be the right decisions. These quick jumps in our thinking can lead us to make poor judgments or bad decisions.

When you are problem solving and hunting for insights, these cognitive shortcuts might lead you to define the wrong problem. This is because your understanding and sense-making is being propelled by your agenda, biases, assumptions or underlying beliefs that have been developed based on your previous experiences.

In a nutshell:

Assumptions

might cause you to only look for valuable problems within your assumptions, yet a valuable problem might come from challenging your assumptions.

Bias

might cause you to discard information if it doesn't support your hypotheses. We are prone to many types of cognitive bias. A common one that inhibits the problem finding process is confirmation bias. This is our tendency to deliberately search for and recall information or problems that confirm our hypotheses or beliefs.

Beliefs

influence you by shaping the way you look for problems or draw conclusions about the world to fit with your reality. Your beliefs and values have the ability to cloud your objectivity in looking for clues and finding problems to solve.

Your agenda, assumptions, biases and beliefs shape the reality of the world you see. To have empathy with your customers, to understand their needs and motivations, you must first have an awareness of these assumptions, biases and beliefs.

So ask yourself the following questions:

What am I assuming that I might not need to?

What do I think I know that might not be the current reality?

What are my hypotheses?

What do I want to know that I don't know?

What do I believe strongly in?

As Bruce Lee once said, 'Empty your mind, be formless, shapeless – like water. Now you put water into a cup, it becomes the cup, you put water into a bottle, it becomes the bottle, you put it in a teapot, it becomes the teapot. Now water can flow or it can crash. Be water, my friend.'

LESSONS FROM THE LAW

It's really hard to explain how I operate – it's just being curious, wanting to know, asking questions, making sure the story makes sense.

When people act out of character, you pick it up and keep asking questions until you can understand why they are reacting the way they are, i.e. are they nervous – why would they be nervous? Why is their story changing?

For example, we responded to a male who had reported a burglary at his house. We asked the victim questions trying to establish what had happened (the facts). How had the offender broken in? What was taken?

The victim reported a large sum of cash and expensive jewellery was stolen. He stated that he left to go to the shops, was absent for two hours and returned to a smashed window and the property stolen.

On inspection, the glass from the broken window was on the outside of the property not the inside, so I wanted to be sure this was the point of entry. On a thorough inspection of the outside of the house, all windows and doors were locked, there were no jemmy marks.

I couldn't establish if a crime had been committed. The victim was nervous and his story kept changing. I detailed my observation to the male – that I couldn't find a point of entry and that if the glass was broken by someone standing outside the house, the broken glass should be on the inside not outside – he confessed to the crime.

He was a gambler and had smashed the window from inside the house.

It's intuition, curiosity takes over. You become inquisitive until you're satisfied you understand what happened.

P.B., Police Detective Senior Sergeant.

Looking for outliers

When you are problem finding, it is important to notice not only how different facts or observations fit together, but to also see how data points don't fit together. How do you treat outliers or anomalies? How do you make sense of contradictory facts and observations?

When you uncover a fact that is contrary to a hypothesis, assumption or belief, you are likely to deduce it as an anomaly. We are good at explaining away inconvenient facts. Throughout my undergraduate degree and research career, for example, I learned it was necessary to remove outliers and anomalies in data sets. Outliers are considered extreme data points that follow different patterns to the rest of the data making their validity suspect.

Yet it is these outliers that could be the very clue you need to help understand your most valuable problem.

If you embrace a seemingly contradictory fact or observation, and take the time to understand further, it may lead you to uncover a new aspect of a problem that you had not previously considered. You can learn from facts and observations that don't make sense to you.

Don't be clue-less

I love Elizabeth Gilbert's quote in *Big Magic*: 'I said yes to every single tiny clue of curiosity that I noticed around me.'

By following clues, we listen with our all of our senses to discover facts, observations, and problems we originally did not know about. You never know where clues and insight to your problem will come from.

It only takes one person in the chain of command within an organisation to not pass a clue along, and it doesn't get to the top, leaving the company secluded from a valuable problem that could be the future growth driver of the business.

So how might you look at new ways of gathering clues? How might you celebrate outliers and contradictions? How might you arrange clue finding excursions? How might you celebrate insight finding? What are some extremes or analogous categories you can learn from?

It can start as simply as having coffee, like Catriona Larritt does at Jetstar Airways. She has a catch-up with someone different in the organisation every day. 'I'm curious about other people. It also helps build connections and solve issues.'

The organisations and leaders that pay attention to the clues are more likely to understand the problems they are trying to solve, and therefore, find the most valuable problems to solve and have greater innovation success.

Don't you want that to be you?

ARE YOU A SLEUTH?

Do you notice things that are not obvious to others?

Do you inquisitively and persistently look for clues?

Does your curiosity provoke you to investigate further or to wonder what is going on?

Do you look for contradictions? When you say to yourself, 'That can't be right?', does this invite you to inquire and investigate further?

Do you look in places for clues others might not have considered?

Do you listen and gather insights with your eyes, not just your ears?

Do you look to learn from disconnects between what people say and do?

Do you walk in others' shoes to get a visceral sense of other people's experiences?

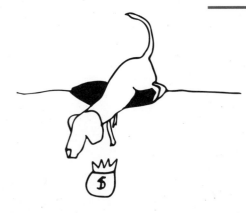

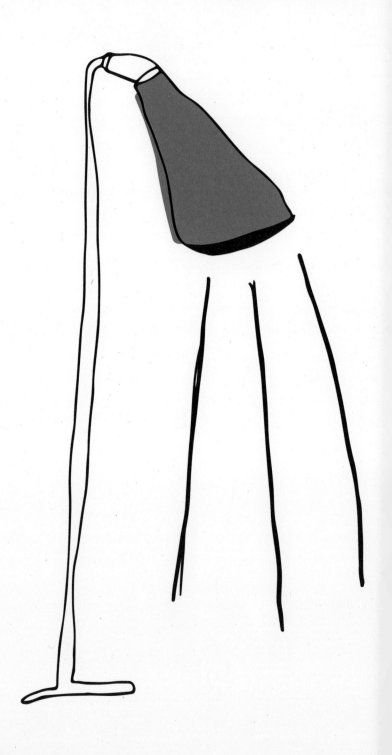

MINDSET 5
INTERROGATOR

'Judge a man by his questions rather than by his answers.'

Voltaire

I have always admired Australian comedian, TV producer and presenter Andrew Denton. He has an uncanny ability to facilitate engaging and deeply touching interviews with both high-profile people, including Bill Clinton, Cate Blanchett, Geoffrey Rush, Bono, Paul Kelly, Raelene Boyle, as well as ordinary people who do extraordinary things.

His interviews are conducted in comfy lounge chairs angled towards each other so Denton and his interviewee can look each other in the eye, with enough space for the interviewee to look away if needed.

Denton clearly does his research. He knows deeply personal details about his interviewees and their lives (including their childhoods), which he uses to connect and build rapport. Through personal sharing and self-deprecation, he creates a mutual sense of status, from which he cultivates a conversation between equals.

Denton has a stillness to his style. His energy and body language never get in the way of his interviews. Yet he displays intense attention to the interviewee, slightly leaning forward, using reassuring smiles. I have observed him placing his hand on his face or chin on many occasions, which to me conveys to the interviewee, 'I'm curious, tell me more ...'

The questions are carefully chosen. They are like a giant spiral, starting outside with safer questions and slowly moving inwards towards the deeply personal and emotional questions, which usually unravel interviewees, once they are warmed up and off guard. I have noticed Denton never asks people how something made them feel. Instead he listens to a story and then paraphrases it back to the interviewee, 'That must have felt ...'

At no point does Denton ever seem like he's following a script. There isn't a formula of questions he uses interview after interview – aside from the use of open-ended questions who, how, when, what, and why. He asks clarifying questions for further understanding, 'What does that mean?' or 'How do you do that ...?' And he doesn't let anyone off the hook. If someone is trying to avoid a question he wants answered, he will simply push and ask it again, 'So I will ask again ...'

It is rare to hear Denton interrupt interviewees. Instead he waits for a pause before asking his next question. He makes provocative statements or asks difficult questions using a gentle, nurturing, non-judgmental tone. In an interview with criminal Mark 'Chopper' Read, Denton says, 'I'm not trying to get you to apologise, I'm trying to drive at who you are now. And the question is, for everybody watching, do you deserve your place back in society? Can you be trusted?' In an interview with politician Pauline Hanson he states, 'In many people's eyes you are a racist ...'

His interviews finish with the sense that the interviewee is Denton's friend rather than someone who has been put under a spotlight. This is quite an achievement given how deeply he delves.

All of these skills are the trademarks of a great interrogator.

Ultimately, Andrew Denton is trying to get to what every problem solver is trying to achieve – which is to arrive at a basic human truth.

Challenge assumptions

Whenever I start a new problem finding project with clients, one of the key questions I pose is, 'What might you be assuming about the challenge that might or might not be true?' I typically gather a very long list of assumptions. People often base assumptions on previous events with similar outcomes.

There are no guarantees of anything. Yet we move through our daily life assuming what we know or what is going to happen. Without realising it, we restrict our thinking by making these unsubstantiated assumptions.

IT'S OUR FAILURE
to be an interrogator

that leads us to the many assumptions that permeate organisations.

Organisations that make assumptions without verifying or challenging what's assumed, end up building walls around their thinking. This results in tackling the same problems with little impact or asking the same questions over and over again.

Failing to encourage a culture of inquiry, where people are free to explore and question, leads to organisations failing to uncover new insights and finding the right problems to solve. This ultimately results in organisations solving the wrong problems.

We must learn and encourage others to ask questions that challenge the status quo and our pervasive beliefs and assumptions. Don't accept the assumed truths for what they are.

Remember, once upon a time we assumed the world was flat!

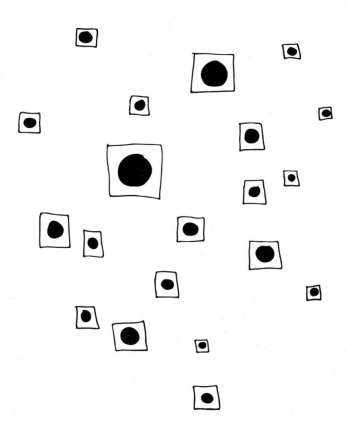

ASSUMPTIONS CONSTRAIN THINKING, SHUT DOWN CONVERSATIONS LIMIT POSSIBILITIES AND INHIBIT PROBLEM FINDING BEHAVIOUR.

FLIP IT

On a blank sheet of paper list all the assumptions you have about a specific problem or challenge. Then reverse each assumption.

For example, let's look at the Apple store prior to the introduction of the Genius Bar. Imagine they had been thinking about how they might improve the in-store customer experience.

Consumers often complained about the after-sales service experience with different mobile manufacturers. For example:

I don't know how to use my device.

I've damaged my device.

My device is broken and needs repairing.

My battery doesn't seem to be charging properly.

So what assumptions about the in-store experience might have been made?

Apple might have listed the following assumption: 'We assume tech-support happens outside of the retail store'.

But what happens if we flip this assumption: 'We assume tech-support happens inside the retail store'.

So when it comes to problem solving and addressing customer pain points, the solutions that emerge by flipping the assumption such as providing tech-support inside the store completely changes the scope of possibilities.

Flipping how you view your situation can lead to an innovative way of identifying a valuable problem to solve.

Four steps to an interrogation

So what does it mean to be an interrogator? How do you become one to help you find and solve problems?

There are four stages involved:

1. Build rapport.

2. Question and pause.

3. Listen deeply.

4. Provoke.

1. Build rapport

The interrogator spends time building a sense of trust and rapport – this is necessary for a mutually enjoyable conversation to occur.

An interrogator seeks out an authentic interaction, building rapport through genuine curiosity and interest. Establishing a sense of commonality or shared experiences such as personal interests can help nurture a higher level of connection and rapport. However, you can't force rapport. Once you become pushy or over-step the level of familiarity, rapport will quickly dissipate.

The interrogator will think about the trajectory of questions, not leaping too quickly into tricky topics without any warm-up. Starting with simple questions like, 'How was your weekend? Did you get up to anything interesting?'

The interrogator is conscious of their body language and the non-verbal signals that could impact on their ability to build rapport. Research has shown that behavioural synchrony (body movements that appear coordinated) between interacting strangers helps to build rapport. So mirroring the body movements of a person you are talking to may help you to build rapport.

Lowering your status is another way to build rapport. I've gone into people's homes and sat on the floor to lower my status and make them feel more relaxed about a stranger being in their home. Look for a lower sitting chair, keep your arms open, lean forward, tilt your head forward, sit in a chair next to the person you are speaking with rather than sitting behind a table. Finally, the simplest non-verbal technique to build rapport is to look non-threatening – smile!

Gift giving can also foster rapport as long as it is sincere and without agenda. This can come in many forms – a genuine compliment or a thoughtful but inexpensive material gift.

2. Question and pause

In his book *A More Beautiful Question: The Power Of Inquiry To Spark Breakthrough Ideas*, Warren Berger refers to a question as 'a lever trying to pry open the stuck lid on a paint can'. The right questions can be very powerful and unlock beliefs, motivations, insights, challenges and problems. Asking the wrong question can be like jamming the lid back on the paint can with a hammer, never to open again!

An interrogator likes to ask questions, and knows how to ask the right question.

The interrogator will pose their next question only when there is a natural pause in the conversation. If you interrupt someone mid-sentence, you are effectively communicating to them: 'I need to stop you right there because what you are saying right now is unimportant and what I have to say or ask is more important than you!'

You might ask clarifying questions such as 'Can you tell me more about that?' or 'I'm not sure I understand about ...' Sometimes you may also need to clarify your understanding to ensure you have interpreted it correctly.

Silence is also powerful. You might also intentionally pause to give the conversation space and to propel the dialogue in a new direction. People often feel the need to end awkward silences. Thus creating silences can result in people offering up insights that you would have never expected nor imagined. You can use silence within a conversation to elicit interesting information, just don't overuse it or it will destroy the dynamics and rapport of the conversation.

3. Listen deeply

Have you ever been in a meeting or conversation but were thinking about your next meeting, or an email you need to write? Or perhaps thinking about the next question you were going to ask?

As soon as you start to think about a reply or the next question before a person is finished, you are not fully present and this will interrupt your listening. You will lose some of the information being offered to you, and you will also lose the emotional context of the information.

An interrogator makes an effort to understand others' perspectives (empathy), through reflective listening. They genuinely seek to understand other people's motivations, perspectives or positions. To listen deeply is to block out distractions and convey your interest using both verbal and non-verbal techniques. Nod your head, maintain eye contact, smile, provide reaffirming cues for people to keep talking through the use of 'yes' or 'mm hmm.'

Listen for disconnects between what is being said and the tone in which it is being conveyed. If someone tells you they love something, can you hear that enthusiasm in their voice? Can you see the enthusiasm in their face and their body language? Why are their eyes darting? Is that sweat on their brow?

The interrogator will listen mindfully to the conversation being offered with both their ears and their eyes.

4. Provoke

Are you brave enough to ask the question that everyone is too scared to ask? Do you call out the elephant in the room when you observe incongruence with what you hear or observe?

You can build rapport, question, and listen deeply, but sometimes that is not enough to get to the magical insights. People don't always tell the truth, sometimes intentionally, sometimes unconsciously. The interrogator is a provocateur, they will poke and pry to get to the truth, to tease out the incongruences in a story.

The interrogator relentlessly follows the inconsistencies to probe for an interesting story or the reason behind the disconnect. This is more than just 'why' questioning. It can be about challenging the truth and their version of events around a story. This ultimately leads you down a path to discover better insights.

The interrogator savours the feeling of surfacing a problem or issue no one else has yet unearthed. They spur people to think about stories and conversations in new ways, and encourage them to think more critically about the problem at hand.

Ask the right question

Why do people die? Why can't I have an ice-cream? Why do I have to go to bed? Why? Why? Why? Young kids are full of questions like these.

At first, parents delight in all the whys, proud of their cherub's curiosity, but then we quickly tire of the bombardment of questions. A 2007 study by psychologist Michele Chouinard found that children between the ages of two and five ask one to three questions per minute.

Strangely what kids are not taught in school is how to ask good questions. Instead they are taught to learn the right answers to questions. Research shows that question-asking peaks at age four or five and then steadily drops off into adulthood, where answers become more valued than questions. Yet we know that asking more questions, also results in greater learning.

You need to change your perspective from thinking about the right answer to thinking about the right question to ask. One of the leaders I interviewed for this book, Barb Hyman, told me that she asks her kids, 'What questions did you ask at school today?' She values question-asking as a skill.

'Why' is one of the simplest and most powerful tools you can use to truly understand the root cause of a problem. But don't just ask 'why' once and stop there. It works best when you ask again and again. At a certain point you will reach an abstract need, common to everyone. It can drive understanding to deeper and deeper levels, like the peeling of an onion. Although, being an interrogator is more than just asking 'why', it's about finding all of the right questions to ask, and there are lots of different types. When you ask different questions, you get people to think about their problems in different ways.

Think about problems as a spider's web – there are many strands and it is all inter-connected.

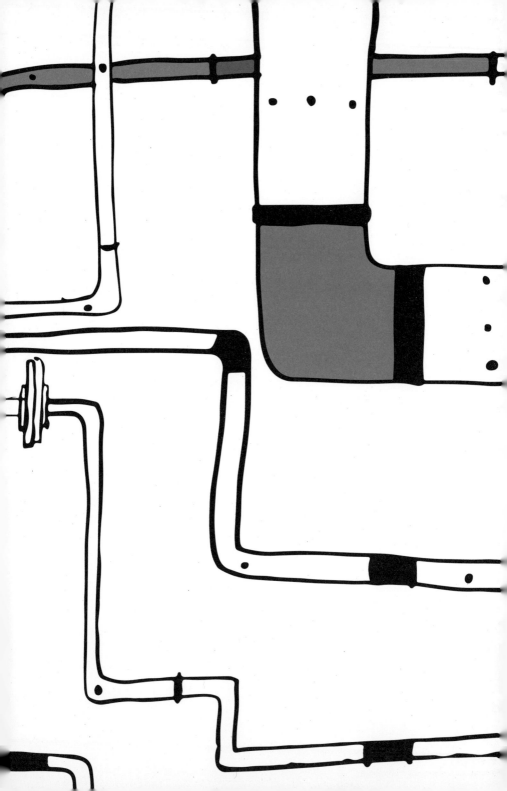

TO
FULLY
UNDERSTAND
A
PROBLEM,

we need to identify all of the threads in the web, and to do this it is not as simple as asking one question.

One of my favourite other questions is 'What's stopping you?' When someone tells you a need or a problem, by simply asking 'What's stopping you?' you get to understand what's stopping someone from satisfying that need. This question helps you to identify where the tension or friction is for customers. By asking this question repeatedly, you will narrow the problem into smaller, task-oriented sub-problems.

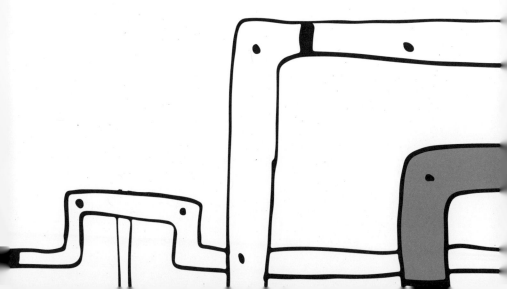

PEELER, FLANKER OR PRISM ?

Dave Gray is the author of *Liminal Thinking*, *The Connected Company* and *Gamestorming*. When I interviewed him for this book, he spoke about different types of questions.

A peeler is a single question that, when repeated, drives attention to deeper and deeper levels, like the peeling of an onion. The purpose of a peeler is to penetrate beyond superficial levels in order to get to the heart of the matter. To move upstream towards a higher-level motivation, you can repeatedly ask the question 'Why?' To move repeatedly downstream towards a more tactical or operational level you can ask 'What's stopping you?'

The purpose of a flanker question is to think laterally and find an analogous situation that may help you think about your problem differently. As Dave explained, 'If you ask a question like "How would you look at this problem if you were a chef in the kitchen?" you are going to get someone looking at the same problem from a completely different perspective, which might give you a new insight.'

A prism is a question that divides problems into smaller groups. Here you can break the problem down into categories or sub-groups. What are the sub-parts of this problem? Dave says, 'If you ask a question like "How does it work?" you are going to get a sequence of events, steps or phases. While a question such as "Can you give me an example of that?" will help you to get a more granular, fleshed-out understanding of your challenge.'

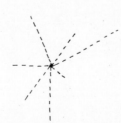

Be persistent

The interrogator has the ability to get beyond obvious or superficial understanding, to uncover deep consumer motivations, beliefs and problems that others have not identified.

When you learn to be an interrogator, you won't put limits on your problem finding behaviour. You'll harvest organisational assumptions, and question and dispel them to open up conversations that explore, discover and test the limits of possibility.

Your insights will help you understand your customers, the decisions they make and the actions they take. This is how you will define everyday problems and identify the future growth drivers of your business.

ARE YOU AN INTERROGATOR?

Do you listen carefully to understand fully before jumping to conclusions or making judgment?

Do you challenge assumed truths?

Do you look to craft and ask the right questions?

Do you engage in a conversation with the intention of learning something new beyond your agenda?

Do you listen more than you talk (even if you are asking questions)? Do you wait for a pause before asking your next question?

Do you ask the question 'why'?

Do you dare to ask questions that others are too scared to ask?

Do you tenaciously follow an interesting story to uncover someone's real thoughts, feelings and behaviours?

MINDSET 6
PLAY-MAKER

'You can discover more about a person in an hour of play than in a year of conversation.'

Plato

Let's play a game.

You have 60 seconds to say out loud all of the things you love.
I'll go first:

I love my kids to the moon and back

I love my husband

I love my parents

I love summer time

I love the endorphins after a run

I love dipping my toes in the ocean

I love the smell of the ocean

I love the feeling of my feet on hot sand

I love it when I catch a wave surfing

I love walking along the street in autumn and kicking the leaves

I love the sound of rain hitting a tin roof

I love the crackle of an open fire

I love the taste of my first coffee of the morning

I love chocolate

I love watching the sunset

I love hanging out with friends

I love listening to music

I love learning something new

I love meeting new people

I love to be challenged

I love the smell of freshly cut grass

I love going to places I have never been before

I love singing in the car to the radio (when no one else can hear me)

I love looking at the stars

I love wondering what else in the universe we haven't discovered yet

When you do an activity like this at work, it completely changes the energy in a room – for the better. You learn a great deal of information about someone very quickly. (Look at how much you just learned about me.)

The problem is that we are not used to being playful at work. I wouldn't be surprised if, when I first mentioned the game at the start, you rolled your eyes and groaned. Would that be a standard response if you suggested it in your next team meeting?

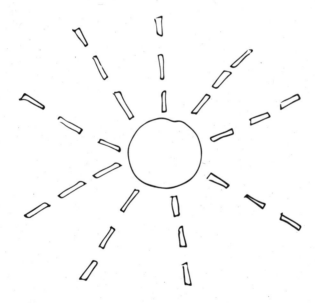

PLAY UNLOCKS COMPLEX PROBLEMS TO SOLVE, AND GIVES US DEEPLY PROFOUND EXPERIENCES.

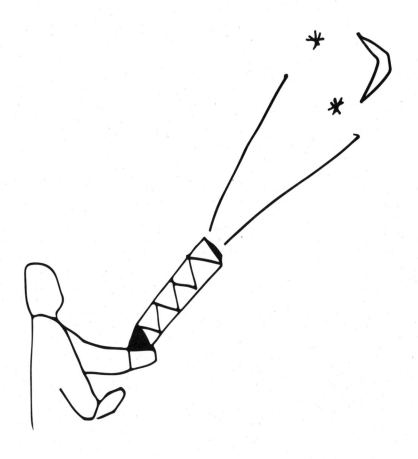

GO SHOPPING

Patrizia Sorgiovanni is a creativity facilitator based in London. Once upon a time she moved to Milan from Canada. She was stepping into a completely foreign cultural environment, as well as into a new role.

Her boss Matteo had an office that looked like a land of colours – a kid's wonderland. There was a big sofa bursting with red, green and yellow pillows. It had floor-to-ceiling bookshelves strewn with books, toy cars, coloured felt, brown string, drums, crayons, pens and a large bag of bouncy balls. On the floor sat an antique-looking brown suitcase completely covered in stamps. There was also a tall treasure chest of toys, each draw filled with cards and pictures. The walls were painted bright yellow and adorned with pops of colour using felt circles. A key feature of the room was the adult finger-painting that hung framed on the wall.

Patrizia could not imagine how Matteo ever got any actual work done.

After a few months in the role she needed to prepare for an upcoming creativity workshop. She was beginning to get a little worried as the deadline was looming.

Patrizia said, 'Okay Matteo, let's start preparing for our workshop. What are we going to do?'

Matteo replied, 'Let's go shopping, there's a great new toy store and I have been meaning to go and see it. It has got all of those old traditional toys made of wood. We have to go, we have to see this!'

Patrizia thought he was mad. 'We have no time to go shopping,' she thought. 'We need to get some work done!'

They walked and talked as they visited stores in and around Milan. She explained: 'We're side by side and he starts to generate some ideas, we could do this and we could do that, and then we get into a store and he picks up a toy and he says we can get the participants to do X, Y and Z, just based on what he saw in that toy.'

They went to several toyshops and walked out with bags of toys. Then suddenly she realised, by the time they returned to the office they had designed the entire workshop. They were done.

Working with someone like Matteo had a profound impact on Patrizia. 'It allowed me to experience and see firsthand the necessity of play,' she says. 'Over the years I started to see how much fun that is and how you don't have to just keep your head down and work like mad and play later. Work and play can be one thing.'

Let's play

When you see a successful leader how often do you think, 'Wow, they must play a lot'?

It is widely acknowledged that kids learn to make sense of the world through play, yet the concept of play in organisations is still pretty new. Many organisations perceive play as a frivolous activity meant for young children, not serious career-driven adults. Play is usually seen as something we do for enjoyment and recreation rather than for a serious or practical purpose.

Yet, science proves that there are many social, emotional and cognitive benefits of play no matter what your age or where you're practising it.

Dr. Sivasailam (Thiagi) Thiagarajan is the founder and Resident Mad Scientist (a true title!) at The Thiagi Group, an American organisation with the mission of helping people improve their performance effectively and enjoyably. Thiagi says:

Organisations are frightened of play for fear of looking silly and not being taken seriously. They think playing is the opposite of being successful. Most organisations are already consciously playing games they are just pretending not to. Most organisations don't realise that play is actually a source of creativity and a tool for problem solving.

Using play for problem finding requires getting employees and leaders to be vulnerable and to step outside of their comfort zones to examine the organisation and its fundamental challenges.

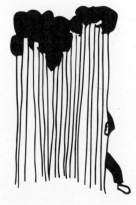

We tend to **FEAR PLAY IN AN ORGANISATION,** for fear of being exposed, looking silly or damaging our personal brand.

Are you serious?

When I mentioned the words 'LEGO Serious Play' to Jake, a client and middle manager in a large corporate organisation, his face said it all.

'I am okay with you using the words "strategy workshop" just take out the word LEGO,' he said about the slides we were preparing for senior management.

Leaders in organisations typically react to any concept of play in one of three ways:

1. This is silly, how can it be productive and worth my time.

2. This is intimidating, I feel nervous.

3. This is awesome, let's get started.

Sure, silly play does not relate to curiosity, nor does it lead to innovation. There is play that exists for play's sake, and many organisations will use play for team building and bonding. But this is not the play I am talking about.

There are many different ways to use play when you're trying to find a valuable problem to solve, including as a tool to:

Teach empathy

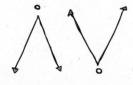

Transition to a focused or divergent task

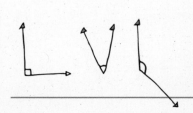

Look at problems from different angles

Debate contentious or critical issues

Navigate uncertainty or possibilities without the stigma of failure

Understand and define complex problems with the use of artefacts and 3D models

Play needs to have a clear purpose where everyone is working towards a shared goal.

The best outcomes are generated when play is built on trust and everyone is a willing participant. This means the set-up and framing of all sessions is critical. It takes time for people to switch out of their serious work day and into a playful mode. It is just like playing sport, you need to do a warm-up to get the most out of your performance.

Play is usually fast, relying more heavily on response from our unconscious brain, which is autonomous, efficient and requires little energy or attention. In play, we simply don't have the time for a slow and controlled way of thinking.

When we get it right, play allows us to go deeper with the insights it unearths. Play can lead us to 'I didn't know I knew that' moments, bringing unconscious knowledge into consciousness.

CURIOSITY & JOY IN A BLENDER

Truly innovative companies don't care about basic skills or levels of degrees. Instead they want to know if you have idea fluency, flexibility and originality (such as knowing all the possible uses of bubble wrap).

Ask yourself:

What is the most playful thing you have ever done at work?

When was the last time you played?

How do you give other people permission to play?

Science shows us that our brain releases dopamine during play, which makes us feel good in the same way that curiosity stimulates the reward system of our brain. We are more creative when we are happy, which means we are more likely to find and solve our most valuable problems.

When you enter into play, you must agree to temporarily suspend reality and engage in behaviour that might be risky, uncomfortable or contentious in everyday work life. In play, leaders aren't expected to have all the answers, everyone plays and everyone contributes, creating a level playing field.

Play will strip away ego, hierarchy and rules to enable 100% participation from everyone in an organisation.

Sometimes I create a dragon's den at the end of a workshop, where I actually make senior executives dress up in children's dragon suits! A dragon's den immediately changes the energy of the room. The dynamic creates excitement, inviting dialogue between the dragons and presenters.

As author of Curious, Todd Kashdan, puts it:

Play is curiosity and joy in a blender ... in play we experiment with different social behaviours, rules and roles. We expand our toolbox of how to relate to other people and what we learn about ourselves. Play is a training ground for change.

Tools for toys

I was facilitating a problem finding session with a client and a number of senior executives. They were all responsible for making decisions about customer problems, but many of the executives weren't connected into the day-to-day frontline issues facing their customers.

I started the workshop using the Empathy Toy, a tool comprising abstract wooden puzzle pieces, each with different textures, colours and shapes that connect into hundreds of possible combinations.

The game starts when one player is given a pre-made pattern. They must explain this pattern to another player (with loose identical pieces) so that they can re-create that exact pattern.

Sounds pretty simple, right?

Not if both of the players are blindfolded.

They can use only words to describe these abstract shapes, so players must create a common language between them. The result is that they gain huge insights into how to communicate better and also create empathy.

Any remaining players are observers who can see, but cannot speak.

What I witnessed was both frustration and patience as my clients tried to work out how to creatively communicate to someone else who couldn't see what they saw. (Ironically this was the reality of their day-to-day work in the call centre communicating with customers on the other end of the phone.)

You don't have to have beanbags, foosball tables and ping-pong to play in your organisation.

The best forms of play do not require elaborate tools, techniques or technology.

All it requires is you – and sometimes a post-it note or two. Remember kids in the playground don't need anything but themselves to create a game to play.

I often play a game (I learnt from Thiagi) where I ask workshop participants to clap after I say 'clap'. But I'll clap my hands before I say the word 'clap'. I trick them into clapping their hands sooner than I have instructed them to. It helps to get people connected to the here and now, and breaks down any barriers.

Our actions speak louder than words.

Think with your hands

You can use the whole body to play, including your hands.

A 2016 experiment by Professor of Organisational Behaviour Gaelle Vallee-Tourangeau explored the effect of interactivity on problem insight. Participants were asked to solve the following problem: how do you put 17 animals in four enclosures in such a manner that there is an odd number of animals in each of the four pens?

Participants were randomly assigned to two group conditions – a tablet and model group. Participants in the tablet group were each given an electronic tablet and a stylus, which they could use to sketch a solution. Participants in the model group were given four metal hoops and 17 animal figurines. They were required to build a model of their solution.

Approximately 17% of the tablet group solved the problem, while 54% of the model group solved the problem, highlighting the benefit of using artefacts in the problem solving process.

Play is fun and energising. It is a mindset that can prepare us for ambiguity and keep us open to opportunities. It can surprise us the most with the insights it unearths.

As British sociologist David Gauntlett said about tactile creative play activities:

Through making things and sharing them with others, we feel a greater connection with the world, and are more engaged with being more active in the environment rather than sitting back and watching.

PLAYGROUND ANTICS

Room set-up and environment is important when you're running a workshop on finding problems or coming up with creative solutions. As Mad Scientist Thiagi explains:

I once instructed a workshop group to draw a diagram of anything they wanted. I gave one half of the room lined graph paper and fine pens capable of drawing tiny lines. For the other half, I gave them torn pieces of blank paper with boxes of crayons. The people with the graph paper and fine pens drew flowcharts and engineering diagrams, while the ones with crayons drew things that reminded them of a playful time in their life.

That's why I will often wrap butcher's paper around the tabletops and lay out pens, crayons and pipe cleaners. So that as we're working through the day in a workshop, people can colour in and scribble notes (doodling has been found to improve information recall by 29%). It gives a much more tactile, kinaesthetic feel to the session.

In any workshop, I'll have lots of different materials: LEGO, clay, Play-Doh, Post-it notes, string and popsicle sticks. We also use our bodies and jump around.

I get a lot of looks from the people in offices nearby on my floor because they wonder what on earth is going on.

Do you facilitate an environment like this for play?

Role play

I was engaged by a leading global retailer to better understand the future needs of their customers across several cities. We used a role-playing tool called Body Storming, which is a technique of physically experiencing, observing or testing a situation to clarify a challenge.

In each lab we invited six customers who had been visiting the client's retail store to participate. I explained the activity to participants in the following way:

In this next activity we are going to have some fun by role-playing different reasons for going to the retail store. This is going to feel a bit stressful and time pressured and that's okay. Don't worry, we are not looking for any budding actors; the aim is to prototype how your experience could work for you in the future.

I then introduced common scenarios to participants. For example, you find out a new product is available and you are interested in buying it, but you first need more information.

The instructions provided to the group were as follows:

> There are six roles to be assigned to the team – two actors, one narrator, two objects and one of any choice. You have five minutes to decide which roles you will play.

> The narrator will provide direction for the actors. Imagine it is like watching TV and you have a remote control. You can move the scene along, freeze it, rewind, stop and start over.

> Objects can have thoughts and feelings and can talk. They can verbalise what is happening at all stages through the narrator.

As the group played out the scenario I intermittently would pause or rewind the scene if I wanted to explore something further. However, what I also threw into the scene were problems a client called 'wrinkles'. They weren't big enough problems to halt the service experience, but they caused enough tension to create a change in behaviour. It allowed us to explore the needs and pain points by crafting a pretend future state.

Body Storming is a sense-making activity and is conducted with real customers. It allows you to witness actual behaviour, rather than typical or staged behaviour, like that in mock role plays with one person pretending to be a customer and another pretending to be an employee.

It embeds you in actual events, behaviours, and problems, so you can better understand work flow inefficiencies, problems to work around, moments of joy and areas for improvement.

When a kid dresses up as a firefighter they are trying on that identity. They want to know what it feels like to be a firefighter. We can do the same thing with play, we are trying on these experiences. The idea of Body Storming is as an empathy tool to better understand the problems we are trying to solve.

As author Dave Gray describes:

There's this whole suspension of reality when you enter a playful space. We know it's just a game and we know we're just playing. Another way of thinking about play is as a simulation. When you look at little kids having a tea party or playing in a playhouse or playing with dolls, or playing sports, they are always in a way simulating some other activity.

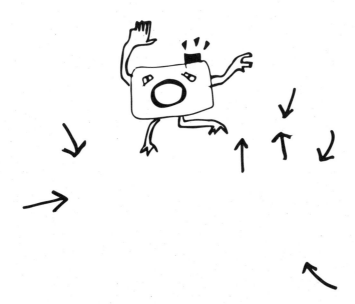

GAME ON

Revisit some of the playful activities in this book. Try them out in your own organisation with your team.

INTRODUCTION
Try your own version of the bullseye game. (Page 10)

RECOGNISE – NOT REWARD
Challenge your team to a problem finding game like John Mars did. (Page 49)

MINDSET 1: Rebel
Create a weekly Vuja De Challenge like that described by Adam Grant. (Page 82)

MINDSET 2: Zen-master
See if your team is paying attention. (Page 112)

MINDSET 3: Novice
Try out the Expert Bees game. (Page 132)

MINDSET 4: Sleuth
Step into the shoes of one of your key customers (limit your spending to what they spend, or eat what they eat), similar to what Coles did. (Page 157)

MINDSET 5: Interrogator
Practise your interrogator skills on a colleague, friend or family member. (Page 176)

MINDSET 6: Play-maker
Try Body Storming for some fun. (Page 212)

Basketball rules

In basketball, you work as a team to try to win the game. You compete against other teams with the goal of being the best. Sound a lot like your organisation?

There is a playbook in basketball. In fact, someone has put together a book called *The Encyclopaedia Of Plays* with over 7,700 plays. This basketball playbook comprises a compilation of strategies a team could use during games. National Basketball Association (NBA) teams commonly have an offensive playbook based on 50 to 60 of these types of plays. There is no formula, teams try out different plays, some work and other don't. They continually keep experimenting and learning.

Phil Jackson, a former American professional basketball player, coach (winning 11 NBA titles) and executive in the NBA, used the triangle offense system with his team, a controversial tool (much like using tools like play within organisations for problem solving), to inject a sense of freedom in the team's play.

In his book *Eleven Rings: The Soul of Success*, Phil explained:

What attracted me to the triangle was the way it empowers the players, offering each one a vital role to play as well as a high level of creativity within a clear, well-defined structure ... With the triangle you can't stand around and wait for the Michael Jordon's and Kobe Bryant's of the world to work their magic. All five players must be fully engaged every second – or the whole system will fail. That stimulates an ongoing process of group problem solving in real time, not just on a coach's clipboard during time-outs.

Play can create a safe environment to uncover and debate critical and contentious issues without consequence. To play out and co-create scenarios or work flows quickly with customers without risk, to test and learn without significant investment, and to use your creativity and imagination to envision a complex future state.

Play shifts our mindset towards experimentation, where you can quickly adapt and go in the direction of what's working without the risk of failure.

Tag, you're it

Soccer icon David Beckham says that he builds LEGO to relax. Comedian Ellen DeGeneres playfully pranks her TV guests. While David Cameron, when he was Britain's Prime Minister, was known to unwind with video games Fruit Ninja and Angry Birds. So you see, it can pay to play, no matter what your job role or status is.

The best way to play is to learn through experience. Start putting some of these playful skills into practice. It is not something you can just think about; you actually need to do it!

Jump in, try things out. Experimenting is never perfect the first time, and that is okay. Invent your own games, or adapt some of the ones from this book. The most important thing is to have fun.

Now it's your turn to play.

ARE YOU A PLAY-MAKER?

Are you open to new experiences?

Do you make 'yes, let's!' your guiding principle?

Do you see the world through a child's eyes?

Do you create a trusted and safe environment to take risks and to play with your team?

Do you play with purpose, where you design and frame work sessions using appropriate games?

Do you surround yourself with playful people?

MINDSET
ROADMAP

'We keep moving forward, we keep opening new doors and doing new things, because we are curious and curiosity keeps leading us down new paths.'

Walt Disney

In this book, you have been introduced to six curiosity mindsets that you can cultivate to help identify your most valuable problems and the future growth drivers of your business. But simply saying that you are curious is not enough to realise the benefits of what you have just read.

The more you can expand your knowledge, the greater impact you will have in your business. Think about curiosity as a muscle you need to develop and exercise. How can you incorporate some of the activities you have read into your everyday work life?

Curiosity is a journey not a destination. Your real expedition starts now.

Here are some suggestions for how you might begin.

Instructions
Pick one mindset at a time to work on – one that you have the most energy for.

REBEL

Ask the question,
'Why is this done this way?'

Pay attention to three novel or unique aspects of an activity that you haven't noticed before.

Invite the dissidents into your organisation and into your workshops.

Create your own organisational rebel-festo.

Search for elephants – have a symbol to represent this (I have a big LEGO elephant I throw into LEGO® SERIOUS PLAY® workshops).

Create your own 'Standing up to status quo' award.

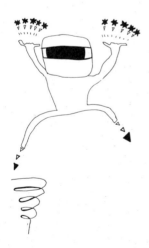

ZEN-MASTER

Count how many times you refrain from checking your phone or thinking about something else in your next meeting.

Pause for a few minutes to tune in and notice your breath.

Give your full attention to mundane tasks like the texture and feel of a door handle you touch to open.

Become a single-tasker and switch tasks only when you are ready to – turn off notifications on your devices.

Block out space in your diary for curious moments.

Play the 'Are you paying attention?' game to bring awareness to your team.

NOVICE

Question whether you really know everything.

Leave your ego at the door of your next meeting.

Keep asking seemingly silly questions.

Challenge yourself to see what you can learn about the person sitting next to you at your next conference.

Try the exercise 'Unlearn the learning' with your team.

Practise having a beginner's mind.

SLEUTH

Stop looking, start observing.

Keep a journal of the tiny moments you notice around you, and record what you see, hear and experience.

Remember, what people say, ain't necessarily what they do.

Step into your customers' shoes to gather clues.

Be aware of assumptions, bias or limiting beliefs.

Conduct weekly coffee catch-ups with someone different in your organisation.

Look for outliers and anomalies and bring those into the problem finding conversation.

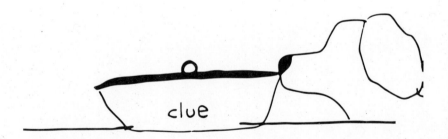

clue

INTERROGATOR

Encourage a culture of inquiry.

Flip all the assumptions you have about a problem.

Ask someone to explain why they have just said 'no' to whatever you have just asked.

Build rapport, question and pause, listen deeply, and provoke in your conversations.

Ask 'why'? A lot.

Be persistent in your quest for truth.

PLAY-MAKER

Pack a playful attitude at work and see what happens.

Try something that you have never done before.

Say, 'yes, let's!' and let curiosity be your guide.

Create a playful environment for your next problem solving session.

Revisit the games and exercises in this book and try them for yourself.

Have fun!

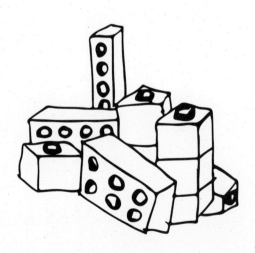

WHERE NEXT?

'Not all those who wander are lost.'

J.R.R. Tolkien

This book has been a learning journey for me, as well as you.

I have been through my own process of unlearning, learning, breaking habits and letting go of old beliefs to help cultivate the gift of curiosity.

During this process, I've had the privilege to meet and have curious conversations with so many outstanding and inspiring individuals – but there is one last story that I would like to share from Daryl Bussell.

One day, I was dropped off somewhere and I thought 'I'll just get the train home and then I'll run from the station to my house.'

I thought it would be an interesting way to learn more about my local community, running from different spots. I had a route I would run on a regular basis, but I'd see the same corners all the time and the same streets, so I was looking for a bit of variety.

I thought if I run from the local station home, and then the next station's only two kilometres further, so I did about three and was sitting there one night talking with my wife, and I said 'I wonder how many stations there are in Melbourne? I wonder if I could run them all.'

I became curious.

There are 209 stations and the furthest one is 52 kilometres away, which isn't that big a deal to me, because I've run much further than that, but I wondered if I could do it within two years?

I have the same goal for each station, but the starting point is always different, and so is the solution, the route that I take. It's the curiosity aspect of my personality that needs to solve each different route, which includes working out the logistics of how I'll get there, directions to get home, where I'll get drinks, what the weather conditions or traffic issues are, and, of course, making sure I don't get lost.

You get the benefit of fitness, you get the benefit of seeing all sorts of different places and often when I'm in conversation people say, 'Are you doing anything interesting at the moment? Are you running a marathon or anything?' I say, 'Funny you should ask that ...'

Most people say, 'That's a great idea. I'd love to do that myself.' I say, 'Well, have a crack!'

Daryl really is the quintessence of curiosity. His leadership style inspires others to be curious every single day.

Awakening your curiosity can truly help you to step out of your current reality to widen your perspectives. And can give you experiences you wouldn't have had otherwise.

Ask yourself, is there a personal curiosity challenge you could now set for yourself?

If you learn only one thing from this book, I hope it's this: curiosity is not an event, it's a daily practice, it's a way of living. Learn to live a curious life. When you embrace the six mindsets you will become more curious, and the more curious you become the more you will learn, experience, discover and grow.

Curiosity is the most powerful thing you own, so let it be your guide.

Evette

Sources

FIND – Don't solve

Kitchen Nightmares, Episode 82, 'Amy's Baking Company' (2013), TV program, Fox Broadcasting Company, Scottsdale, Arizona, USA.

Wedell-Wedellsborg, T. (2017), 'Are you solving the right problems?' *Harvard Business Review*, pp. 2–9.

Basadur, M.S. (1992), 'Managing creativity: A Japanese model', *The Academy of Management Executive*, 6(2), pp. 29–42.

Basadur M.S., Wakabayashi, M. & Takai J. (1992), 'Training effects on the divergent thinking attitudes of Japanese managers', *International Journal of Intercultural relations*, 16(3), pp. 329–345.

Basadur, M.S., Graen, G.B. & Green, S.G. (1982), 'Training in creative problem solving: Effects on ideation and problem finding in an applied research organization', *Organizational Behavior and Human Performance*, 30, pp. 41–70.

Basadur, M.S. (editor, Runco, M.A.) (1994), 'Managing the creative process in organizations', in *Problem finding, problem solving and creativity*, chapter 12, Ablex, New York.

Basadur, M.S., Pringle, P.F., Speranzini, G. & Bacot, M. (2000), 'Collaborative problem solving through creativity in problem definition: Expanding the pie', *Creativity and Innovation Management*, 9(1), pp. 54–76.

Basadur, M.S., Ellspermann, S.J. & Evans, G.W. (1994), 'A new methodology for formulating ill-structured problems', *OMEGA: The International Journal of Management Science*, 22(6), pp. 627–645.

Lebowitz, S. (2017), 'Google and Facebook still use the 3-word question that saved a $225 billion company in the 1970s', *Business Insider*.

Parnes, S.J. (1967), *Creative Behavior Guidebook*, Scribners, New York.

Basadur, M. (1992), *Flight to Creativity*, Creative Education Foundation, Canada.

Berger, W. (2012), 'The secret phrase top innovators use', *Harvard Business Review*, pp. 2–9.

Kashdan, T. (2010), *Curious? Discover the Missing Ingredient to a Fulfilling Life*, Harper Collins, USA.

Getzels, J.W. (1975), 'Problem-finding and the inventiveness of solutions', *The Journal of Creative Behavior.*

2. RECOGNISE – Don't reward

Henneberg, M., Lambert, K.M. & Leigh, C. (1997), 'Fingerprinting a chimpanzee and a koala: Animal dermatoglyphics can resemble human ones', *Natural Science.*

Berlyne, D.E. (1954), 'A theory of human curiosity', *British Journal of Psychology*, 45, pp. 180–191.

Kidd, C. & Hayden, B.Y. (2015), 'The psychology and neuroscience of curiosity', *Neuron*, 88, November, pp. 449–460.

Loewenstein, G. (1994), 'The psychology of curiosity: A review and reinterpretation', *Psychological Bulletin*, 116, pp. 75–98.

Kang, M.J., Hsu, M., Krajbich, I.A., Loewenstein, G., McClure, S.M., Tao-yi Wang, J. & Camerer, C.F. (2009), 'The wick in the candle of learning: Epistemic Curiosity Activates Reward Circuitry and Enhances Memory', *Psychological Science*, 20, pp. 963–973.

Gruber, M.J., Gelman, B.D. & Ranganath, C. (2014), 'States of curiosity modulate hippocampus-dependent learning via the dopaminergic circuit', *Neuron*, 84, pp. 486–496.

Lohr, S. (2017), 'A new kind of tech job emphasizes skills, not a college degree', *New York Times*

Heifetz, R.A., Linksy, M. & Grashow, A. (2009), *The Practice of Adaptive Leadership: Tools and Tactics for Changing Your Organization and the World*, Cambridge Leadership Associates, USA.

Costa, P.T. Jr. & McCrae, R.R. (1992), *Revised NEO Personality Inventory (NEO PI-R) and NEO Five-Factor Inventory (NEO-FFI): Professional Manual*,

Psychological Assessment Resources, Odessa, FL.

MINDSET 1: Rebel
Asch, S.E. (1955), 'Opinions and social pressure', *Scientific American*, 193(5), pp. 31–35.

Berns., G.S., Chappelow, J., Zink, C.F., Pagnoni, G., Martin-Skurski, M.E. & Richards, J. (2005), 'Neurobiological correlates of social conformity and independence during mental rotation', *Journal of Biological Psychiatry*, 58, pp. 245–253.

Kalb, C. (2016), *Andy Warhol was a Hoarder: Inside the Minds of History's Great Personalities*, National Geographic Books, USA.

Terdiman, D. (2009), *Recollections of the Mac's Creators*, www.CNET.com.

Isaacson, W. (2015), *Steve Jobs*, Simon and Schuster, USA.

Grant, A. (2016), *Originals: How Non-conformists Change the World*, WH Allen, USA.

Bezos, J. (2017), *Letter to Shareholders*, www.Amazon.com.

MINDSET 2: Zen-master
Csikszentmihalyi, M. (1990), *Flow: The Psychology of Optimal Experience*, Harper Collins, USA.

Adler, R.F. & Benbunan-Fich, R. (2013), 'Self-interruptions in discretionary multitasking', *Computers in Human Behavior*, 29, pp. 1441–1449.

Mark, G., Gudith, D. & Klocke, U. (2008), 'The cost of interrupted work: More speed and stress', Conference on Human Factors in Computing Systems (CHI 2008), Florence, Italy, ACM Press, pp. 107–110.

American Psychological Association (2006), *Multitasking: Switching Costs*, www.apa.org.

Killingsworth, M.A. & Gilbert, D.T. (2010), 'A wandering mind is an unhappy mind', *Science*, 330, p. 932.

MINDSET 3: Novice

Lawson, R. (2006), 'The science of cycology: Failures to understand how everyday objects work', *Memory and Cognition*, pp. 1667–1675.

Rozenblit, L. & Keil, F. (2002), 'The misunderstood limits of folk science: An illusion of explanatory depth', *Cognitive Science*, 26, pp. 521–562.

Ottati, V., Price, E.D., Wilson, C. & Sumaktoyo, N. (2015), 'When self-perceptions of expertise increase closed-minded cognition: The earned dogmatism effect', *Journal of Experimental Social Psychology*, 61, pp. 131–138.

Thiagarajan, S. (2016), *Looking Around*, www.Thiagi.com.

MINDSET 4: Sleuth

Marshall, B.J., Armstrong, J.A., McGechie, D.B. & Glancy, R.J. (1985), 'Attempts to fulfil Koch's postulates for pyloric campylobacter', *Medical Journal of Australia*, 142, pp. 436–439.

Marshall B.J. (2005), *Barry J. Marshall – Biographical*, www.Nobelprize.org.

Gosling, S.D., Ko, S.J., Mannarelli, T. & Morris, M.E. (2002), 'A Room with a cue: Judgments of personality based on offices and bedrooms', *Journal of Personality and Social Psychology*, 82, pp. 379–398.

Tversky, A. & Kahneman, D. (1974), 'Judgment under uncertainty: Heuristics and biases', *Science*, 185, pp. 1124–1130.

McCauley, D. (2016), *Coles Bosses Get a Rude Awakening After being Challenged to Do a Weekly Shop on a $150 Budget*, www.News.com.

Simons, D.J. & Chabris, C.F. (1999), 'Gorillas in our midst: Sustained inattentional blindness for dynamic events', *Perception*, 28, pp. 1059–1074.

Gilbert, E. (2015), *Big Magic: Creative Living Beyond Fear*, Bloomsbury, UK.

Barnett, V. & Lewis, T. (1994), *Outliers in Statistical Data* (3rd ed.), Wiley, USA.

MINDSET 5: Interrogator
Denton, A. (2007), *Best of Enough Rope: 1001 Interviews You Must Read Before You Die*, ABC Books, Australia.

Berger, W. (2016), *A More Beautiful Question: The Power of Inquiry to Spark Breakthrough Ideas*, Bloomsbury, USA.

Basadur, M. (1995), *The Power of Innovation: How to Make Innovation a Way of Life and Put Creative Solutions to Work*, Pearson Education, UK.

Basadur, M. & Goldby M. (2016), *Design-Centered Entrepreneurship*, Routledge, USA.

Tickle-Degnan, L. & Rosenthal, R. (1990), 'The nature of rapport and its nonverbal correlates', *Psychological Inquiry*, 1(4), pp. 285–293.

Vacharkulksemsuk, M.A. & Fredrickson, B.L. (2012), 'Stranger in sync: Achieving embodied rapport through shared movements', *Journal of Experimental Social Psychology*, 48(1), pp. 399–402.

Abbe, A. & Brandon, S.E. (2013), 'The role of rapport in investigative interviewing: A review', *Journal of Investigative Psychology and Offender*, 10, pp. 237–249.

MINDSET 6: Play
Nussbaum, B. (2013), *Creative Intelligence*, Harper Collins, USA.

West, S., Hoff, E. & Carlsson, I. (2013). 'Playing at work: Professionals' conceptions of the functions of play on organizational creativity', *The International Journal of Creativity and Problem Solving*, 23(2), pp. 5–23.

Brown, S. (2009), *Play: How it Shapes the Brain, Opens the Imagination, and Invigorates the Soul*, Penguin, USA.

Gray, D., Brown, S. & Macanufo, J. (2010), *Gamestorming: A Playbook for Innovators, Rulebreakers, and Changemakers*, O'Reilly Media, USA.

Kashdan, T. (2010), *Curious? Discover the Missing Ingredient to a Fulfilling Life*, Harper Collins, USA.

Andrade, J. (2009), 'What does doodling do?' *Applied Cognitive Psychology*, pp. 100–106.

Oulasvirta, A., Kurvinen, E. & Kankainen, T. (2003), 'Understanding contexts by being there: Case studies in bodystorming', *Personal Ubiquitous Computing*, 7(1), pp. 125–134.

Jackson, P. (2013), *Eleven Rings: The Soul of Success*, Penguin, USA.

Vallée-Tourangeau, F., Vork Steffensen, S., Vallée-Tourangeau, G. & Sirota, M. (2016), 'Insight with hands and things', *Acta Psychologica*, pp. 195–205.

Gauntlett, D. (2011), *Making is Connecting*, Polity Press, UK.

Stay curious.